Understanding
King Lear

The Greenwood Press "Literature in Context" Series

Student Casebooks to Issues, Sources, and Historical Documents

Understanding
King Lear

A STUDENT CASEBOOK TO ISSUES, SOURCES, AND HISTORICAL DOCUMENTS

Donna Woodford

The Greenwood Press
"Literature in Context" Series
Claudia Durst Johnson, Series Editor

GREENWOOD PRESS
Westport, Connecticut • London

1- 2134

Library of Congress Cataloging-in-Publication Data

Woodford, Donna.
    Understanding King Lear : a student casebook to issues, sources, and historical
documents / Donna Woodford.
        p. cm.—(The Greenwood Press "Literature in context" series, ISSN 1074-598X)
    Includes bibliographical references and index.
    ISBN 0–313–31936–7
    1. Shakespeare, William, 1564–1616. King Lear. 2. Shakespeare, William, 1564–1616.
King Lear—Sources. 3. Lear, King (Legendary character), in literature. 4. Inheritance and
succession in literature. 5. Kings and rulers in literature. 6. Britons in literature. 7. Tragedy.
I. Title. II. Series.
PR2819.U54 2004
822.3'3—dc22   2004003576

British Library Cataloging in Publication Data is available.

Library of Congress Catalog Card Number: 2004003576
ISBN: 0–313–31936–7
ISSN: 1074–598X

First published in 2004

Greenwood Press, 88 Post Road West, Westport, CT 06881
An imprint of Greenwood Publishing Group, Inc.
www.greenwood.com

Printed in the United States of America

The paper used in this book complies with the
Permanent Paper Standard issued by the National
Information Standards Organization (Z39.48–1984).

10 9 8 7 6 5 4 3 2 1

This book is dedicated to my grandmother, who bravely endured the storm of old age.

Contents

Contents

Acknowledgments

A book is in many ways a collaborative effort, and many people contributed to the creation of *Understanding King Lear*. I extend my gratitude to Claudia Durst Johnson and Lynn Malloy Araujo for their patience in editing this text and for their insights and suggestions. I also wish to thank Eric Brown for introducing me to the Literature in Context series and for making me aware of the opportunity to write this book. The Folger Shakespeare library has been an invaluable resource to me, and I thank the talented and generous Folger staff for their assistance. I also extend my gratitude to Dr. Nancy Larrick Crosby and the Fund for Excellence for enabling me to spend time working at the Folger Library. My grandmother inspired the last chapter of this book, and her experience with aging gave me new insights about *King Lear*. My parents generously shared their experiences of caring for an aging parent. I gratefully acknowledge the invaluable contributions that all three of them made to this book. I also wish to thank all of the friends, too numerous to mention, who listened to my concerns and offered their ideas and encouragement. I thank Alice and Paul for their unwavering love and loyalty, and I am especially grateful to Chaz Gormley, who has supported and encouraged me throughout this process.

Introduction

King Lear is one of Shakespeare's great tragedies. It incorporates elements of fairy tales, history, and legends, and it alludes to many of the controversial political issues in Shakespeare's day. It appealed to readers then, and continues to appeal to readers now in part because it is both a political and a domestic tragedy; it operates both on a national level and on a very personal, familial level. But *King Lear* can also be a daunting play, especially for first-time readers. Its intricate double plot can be confusing; the topical references may mean little to a modern audience; and we may not, at first, see the relevance of the play to our own times. Studying the play in context can eliminate many of those problems. Understanding the social and political context of Shakespeare's time can illuminate the text. We can better understand the behavior of the characters in *King Lear* if we know how families were expected to behave and how the insane were treated and perceived in the sixteenth and seventeenth centuries. We can understand the topical references in the play if we know something about the political events of the time during which the play was written. Likewise, we can appreciate the relevance of the play today if we look at it a contemporary context. We can compare the treatment of Lear and his relationship with his daughters to the treatment of the elderly today and the difficult decisions about long-term care faced by the elderly and their family members. And we can compare the behavior of Lear to the behavior of Alzheimer's patients. Looking at adaptations of *King Lear,* which often alter the context of the story, can also help us to better understand the play and the issues it presents. Examining a similar story told from a different perspective or set in a different time or place can both raise new issues and show us how the issues raised in *King Lear* are relevant in a variety of different contexts.

This book places *King Lear* in context by providing a wide assortment of documents, including the following:

- speeches and political tracts by King James I
- historical chronicles
- an excerpt from a fairy tale
- legal documents
- letters concerning the custody of an aging father
- conduct books
- medical treatises
- a popular ballad
- excerpts from other plays
- sermons
- book and film reviews
- newspaper articles
- a letter from former President Reagan
- an interview with Alzheimer's caregivers
- a personal account of life with Alzheimer's

Studying these documents alongside *King Lear* will enable students to better understand Shakespeare's play, the time in which it was written, and its continued relevance today. The questions at the end of each section will also encourage students to consider *King Lear* in the context provided by these documents, and the suggested readings will allow students to further explore areas of particular interest. The goal of this book is to make Shakespeare and *King Lear* more accessible to students, while also encouraging them to think about literature in new and creative ways that reach beyond the text and into the many contexts surrounding it.

NOTE

All quotations of *King Lear* in this book are from the conflated text in *The Norton Shakespeare,* Ed. Stephen Greenblatt, et al. (New York and London: W. W. Norton, 1986).

1 _____

Dramatic Analysis

This first chapter will provide an analysis of various dramatic and literary elements of *King Lear*. We will begin by looking at the historical, mythical, and literary sources of the story, examining both the borrowed elements of the plot and the unique contributions and revisions of Shakespeare. Next we will analyze the text, looking for patterns or motifs in the language, imagery, and characters. Finally, we will probe these patterns in order to understand the meaning or the themes of the play. The spelling and punctuation of the documents included in this chapter have been modernized where necessary for the sake of clarity.

A TALE RETOLD

Because Shakespeare is revered by so many people as a creative genius, students may be very surprised to learn that in most cases Shakespeare borrowed the basic plots of his plays from other sources. Sometimes he borrowed from English history; sometimes he borrowed from other plays, poems, or works of fiction. This does not mean that Shakespeare was not a genius, or that he was merely repeating other people's stories. His genius can be seen in the way he adapted the existing stories, changed them and made them into his own masterpieces.

In the case of *King Lear* there were numerous earlier versions of the main story, and the subplot of Gloucester and his sons was also borrowed from another source. The story of King Lear, his test of his three daughters' love for him, and the suffering caused by his misjudgment of their answers had been told in English histories such as Geoffrey of Monmouth's *Historia Regum Britanniae* (*The History of the Kings of Britain*) and Raphael Holinshed's *Chronicles of England, Scotland, and Ireland,* as well as in poems such as *A Mirror for Magistrates* and Edmund Spenser's *The Faerie Queene.* There was also an anonymous play titled *The True Chronicle History of King Leir and His Three Daughters, Gonorill, Ragan and Cordella,* which was probably written in the 1590s, about a decade before Shakespeare's *King Lear,* which was composed around 1605. The story of a king who divides his land among his daughters in return for their promises of love for him is also reminiscent of fairy tales such as the Grimm's fairy tale, *The Goosegirl at the Well.* And the story of Gloucester and his two sons comes from Sir Phillip Sidney's prose romance, *The Countess of Pembroke's Arcadia.* So, clearly, the story would have been well known to Shakespeare and to his audience.

Shakespeare, however, made substantial changes to the well-known story. Though he borrowed both the subplot of Gloucester and his sons and the main plot of King Lear and his daughters, Shakespeare was the first to combine the two stories. Many of his plays weave together a main plot and a secondary story, but *King Lear* is by far his most complicated use of a subplot, the two stories being intricately woven together, and each emphasizing and reinforcing the themes of the other. Shakespeare was also the first to make Lear mad; he introduced the storm scenes, possibly the most memorable scenes of the play; and he added the characters of the Fool and banished Kent. And perhaps most surprisingly for his original audience, he changed the ending of the play. All of the earlier versions of the King Lear story, including the historical chronicles, end with Lear regaining the throne with the assistance of Cordelia and her husband, reigning until his death, and then passing the kingdom on to Cordelia. The ending was still not entirely happy because five years into Cordelia's reign, her nephews, the sons of her sisters, deposed her, causing her to kill herself in despair. But only in Shakespeare's play do we see the starkly tragic ending in which Cordelia, Lear, Goneril, and Regan all die, leaving the royal line extinct and the kingdom without an heir. Shakespeare's original audience must have been as surprised and shocked by this ending as a modern audience would be by a Cinderella story that ends with the prince marrying one of the ugly stepsisters. Nevertheless, while Shakespeare's story may have been somewhat shocking, it is his changes and additions to the original story that make it the masterful tragedy that has lasted 400 years. It is interesting to see what Shakespeare borrowed from other sources, but it is even more interesting to note the changes he made and the effect which those changes have on the play.

HISTORY REWRITTEN

The primary source for the story of King Lear and his daughters, of course, is Britain's legendary past, which in Shakespeare's time was considered factual history. There were many chronicles of English history, but two of the best known, and the two from which Shakespeare is thought to have borrowed the most, are Geoffrey of Monmouth's *History of the Kings of Britain* and Holinshed's *Chronicles of England, Scotland, and Ireland*. Geoffrey of Monmouth claimed to have translated his *History* into Latin from an ancient British text that he had found. Though we now believe that he in fact wrote the history himself, in Shakespeare's day the stories in Geoffrey's *History* were still considered historical fact. Although the Latin text had been written around 1135 A.D., it was still available in Shakespeare's time, and while there were no English translations of the work at that time, Shakespeare may well have read the Latin. Holinshed's *Chronicle* was also widely available in Shakespeare's time and appears to have been the source of many of his history plays. But while Shakespeare may have borrowed much of his plot from these and other historical accounts, he made some significant and surprising changes. In both Geoffrey of Monmouth's and Holinshed's accounts, for example, King Lear tests the love of his daughters and rewards the flattering older daughters while disowning the truthful youngest daughter, but in neither text does he give away his entire kingdom during his lifetime. Rather, he gives his two daughters and their husbands half of his kingdom and promises them the whole kingdom after his death. It is, as the following excerpt of Geoffrey's *History* demonstrates, the treachery of his daughters and their husbands that deprives the historical Lear of his kingdom during his lifetime. By giving the kingdom away himself, Shakespeare's Lear brings about his own tragic end. The Lear of the histories seems less responsible for his own downfall, but he also appears to learn less from it. As his speech at the end of the following excerpt indicates, he is primarily angry at the "grandeur from which he had fallen" and the indignities which he himself has had to suffer, whereas Shakespeare's Lear comes to realize and regret that he has taken "too little care" of his poor subjects (3.4.34).

FROM GEOFFREY OF MONMOUTH, *THE HISTORY OF THE
KINGS OF BRITAIN* (C. 1135), IN *THE BRITISH HISTORY OF
GEOFFREY OF MONMOUTH,* ED. J. A. GILES,
TRANS. A. THOMPSON

(London, 1842)

Book 2, Chapter 12

A long time after this, when Leir came to be infirm through old age, the two dukes, on whom he had bestowed Britain with his two daughters, fostered an insurrection against him, and deprived him of his kingdom, and of all regal authority, which he had hitherto exercised with great power and glory. At length, by mutual agreement, Maglaunus, duke of Albania, one of his sons-in-law, was to allow him a maintenance at his own house, together with sixty soldiers, who were to be kept for state. After two years' stay with his son-in-law, his daughter Gonorilla grudged the number of his men who began to upbraid the ministers of the court with their scanty allowance; and having spoken to her husband about it, gave orders that the number of her father's followers should be reduced to thirty, and the rest discharged. The father, resenting this treatment, left Maglaunus, and went to Henuinus, duke of Cornwall, to whom he had married his daughter Regau. Here he met with an honourable reception, but before the year was at end, a quarrel happened between the two families, which raised Regau's indignation; so that she commanded her father to discharge all his attendants but five, and to be contented with their service. This second affliction was insupportable to him, and made him return again to his former daughter, with hopes that the misery of his condition might move in her some sentiment of filial piety, and that he, with his family, might find a subsistence with her. But she, not forgetting her resentment, swore by the gods he should not stay with her, unless he would dismiss his retinue, and be contented with the attendance of one man; and with bitter reproaches, told him how ill his desire of vain-glorious pomp suited his age and poverty. When he found that she was by no means to be prevailed upon, he was at last forced to comply, and, dismissing the rest, to take up with one man only. But by this time he began to reflect more sensibly with himself upon the grandeur from which he had fallen, and the miserable state to which he was now reduced, and to enter upon thoughts of going beyond sea to his youngest daughter. Yet he doubted whether he should be able to move her commiseration, because...he had treated her so unworthily. However, disdaining to bear any longer such base usage, he took ship for Gaul. In his passage, he observed he had only the third place given him among the princes that were with him in the ship, at which with deep sighs and tears, he burst forth into the following complaint.

"O irreversible decrees of the Fates, that never swerve from your stated course! Why did you ever advance me to an unstable felicity, since the punishment of lost happiness is greater than the sense of present misery? The remembrance of a time when vast numbers of men obsequiously attended me in the taking the cities and wasting the enemy's countries, more deeply pierces my heart, than the view of my present calamity, which has exposed me to the derision of those who were formerly prostrate at my feet. O! the enmity of fortune! Shall I ever again see the day when I may be able to reward those according to their deserts who have forsaken me in my distress? How true was thy answer, Cordeilla, when I asked thee concerning thy love to me, 'As much as you have, so much is your value, and so much do I love you.' While I had any thing to give they valued me, being friends not to me, but to my gifts: They loved me then, but they loved my gifts much more: When my gifts ceased, my friends vanished. But with what face shall I presume to see you, my dearest daughter, since in my anger I married you upon worse terms than your sisters, who, after all the mighty favors they have received from me, suffer me to be in banishment and poverty?" (34–6)

Shakespeare's Lear also dies a more tragic death than the historical Lear. He dies not only having lost his kingdom but also realizing at the end that his own folly has destroyed him and his beloved daughter. The historical Lear, as the following excerpt from Holinshed's *Chronicles* indicates, is able to regain his kingdom, and though Cordelia will eventually be deposed and commit suicide, Lear dies knowing that he is leaving his kingdom to the truest daughter and the rightful heir.

FROM RAPHAEL HOLINSHED, *CHRONICLES OF ENGLAND, SCOTLAND, AND IRELAND*, VOL. 1 (1587)

(London, 1807)

Book 2, Chapter 5

Now when he [Lear] had informed his son in law and his daughter in what sort he had been used by his other daughters, Aganippus caused a mighty army to be put in a readiness, and likewise a great navy of ships to be rigged, to pass over into Britain with Leir his father in law, to see him again restored to his kingdom. It was accorded, that Cordeilla should also go with him to take possession of the land, the which he promised to leave unto her, as the rightful inheritor after his decease, notwithstanding any former grant made to her sisters or to their husbands in any manner of wise.

Hereupon, when this army and navy of ships were ready, Leir and his daughter Cordeilla with her husband took the sea, and arriving in Britain, fought with their enemies, and discomfited them in battle, in the which Maglanus and Henninus were slain: and then was Leir restored to his kingdom, which he ruled after this by the space of two years and then died, forty years after he first began to reign. (447–8)

Chapter 6

This Cordeilla after her father's decease ruled the land of Britain right worthily during the space of five years, in which mean time her husband died, and then about the end of those five years, her two nephews Margan and Cunedag, sons to her aforesaid sisters, disdaining to be under the government of a woman, levied war against her, and destroyed a great part of the land, and finally took her prisoner, and laid her fast in ward, wherewith she took such grief, being a woman of a manly courage, and despairing to recover liberty, there she slew herself, when she had reigned (as before is mentioned) the term of five years. (448)

HISTORY REPEATED

Shakespeare and his contemporaries might have recognized the story of King Lear not only because it was a story out of English history, but also because a recent lawsuit had seemed like a curious echo of the ancient legend. In 1603 a gentleman named Sir Bryan Annesley found himself in a situation much like that of King Lear. Annesley had three daughters: Lady Grace Wildgoose (her married name, also spelled Wildgos, Wildgose, and Willgosse), Christian, and Cordell. Grace and her husband, John Wildgoose, wrote to Sir Robert Cecil, an influential member of the courts of both Queen Elizabeth and King James, and asked him to declare Annesley a lunatic so that they could gain control of his estate. Cordell protested on his behalf and was able to convince the court that her father, after his long years of service to the court, should not be declared insane. When he died Annesley left most of his estate to Cordell, and though the Wildgooses protested the will, it was upheld.

Cordell, of course, resembles Lear's youngest daughter both because their names are remarkably similar and because both loyally defend their fathers when their elder sisters turn treacherous. We cannot know how much the case influenced Shakespeare, though it may well have been familiar to him, but it is interesting because it clearly demonstrates that the issues at the heart of *King Lear* are important not just to legendary kings and princesses, but to ordinary families as well. As the letters from Sir John Wildgoose and from Cordell Annesley show, the ancient legend of King Lear was still relevant to families in Shakespeare's time, and the issues continue to strike a chord with audiences today. The first letter below is from Sir John Wildgoose to Sir Robert Cecil. In it he complains of Cordell Annesley's refusal to allow him to take an inventory of the belongings of Sir Bryan Annesley, belongings which Wildgoose wanted to obtain. The second letter is from Cordell Annesley to Sir Robert Cecil. She thanks him for his assistance and continues to plead with him not to brand her father a lunatic. She also requests that her father, if he must be declared lunatic, be placed in the care of someone who will be more concerned about his well-being than about the money to be made from his estate.

SIR JOHN WILDGOOSE, LETTER TO LORD CECIL (1603), IN HISTORICAL MANUSCRIPTS COMMISSION, *CALENDAR OF THE MANUSCRIPTS OF THE MOST HONORABLE THE MARQUESS OF SALISBURY, HATFIELD HOUSE, HERTFORDSHIRE,* VOL. 15, ED. M. S. GIUSSEPPI

(London: His Majesty's Stationary Office, 1930)

1603, Oct. 18.—According to your letter of the 12th of this present, we repaired unto the house of Bryan Annesley, of Lee, in the county of Kent, and finding him fallen into such imperfection and distemperature of mind and memory, as we thought him thereby become altogether unfit to govern himself or his estate, we endeavored to take a perfect inventory of such goods and chattels as he possessed in and about his house. But Mrs. Cordall, his daughter, who during the time of all his infirmity hath taken upon her the government of him and his affairs, refuseth to suffer any inventory to be taken, until such time as she hath had conference with her friends, by reason whereof we could proceed no farther in the execution of your letter.—From Lee, 18 Oct, 1603.

Signed: John Wildgos, Tymothe Lawe, Samuel Lennard. (262)

CORDELL ANNESLEY, LETTER TO LORD CECIL (OCTOBER 23, 1603), IN CHARLOTTE CARMICHAEL STOPES, *THE LIFE OF HENRY, THIRD EARL OF SOUTHAMPTON, SHAKESPEARE'S PATRON*

(Cambridge: Cambridge University Press, 1922)

I most humbly thank you for the sundry letters that it hath pleased you to direct unto gentlemen of worship in these parts, requesting them to take into their custodies the person and estate of my poor aged and daily dying father. But that course so honorable and good for all parties, intended by your Lo. [Lordship], will by no means satisfy Sr. John Willgosse, nor can any course else, unless he may have him begged for a Lunatic, whose many years service to our late dread Sovereign Mistress and native country deserved a better agnomination, than at his last gasp to be recorded and registered a Lunatic, yet find no means to avoid so great an infamy and endless blemish to us and our posterity, unless it shall please our Lo. Of your honourable disposition, if he must needs be accounted a Lunatic, to bestow him upon Sir James Croft, who out of the love he bare unto him in his more happier days, and for the good he wisheth unto us his children, is contented upon entreaty to undergo the burden and care of him and his estate, without intendment to make one penny benefit to himself by any goods of his, or ought that may descend to us his children, as also to prevent any record of Lunacy that may be procured hereafter. Lewsham, 23, October, 1603.
Cordell Annesley. (274)

FAIRY TALE AND LEGEND

Shakespeare borrowed the story of *King Lear* directly from English legendary history and from poetic and dramatic accounts of English history, but readers of *King Lear* may also recognize some elements of common fairy tales in the play's story. The story of the father who divides his property among his children according to their alleged love for him and then regrets his poor judgment is a tale that had been told in many countries and for many centuries. In Europe it existed in the form of *The Goose Girl at the Well,* one of many fairy tales collected by the Brothers Grimm. In the following excerpt of the story, the mother of the princess tells how her husband, the king, decided to test his daughters' love for him in order to determine what each daughter should inherit after his death. In this story, as in *King Lear,* the father fails to understand the significance of the youngest daughter's speech. When Cordelia says she loves her father "according to [her] bond, no more nor less" she is saying that she loves her father as any daughter should love her father, because he has "begot," "bred," and "loved" her as a father (1.1.92, 95). Likewise when the goose-girl princess says that she loves her father as she loves salt, she is in fact saying that she loves him the way she loves that which gives flavor and taste to life. Both fathers, however, hear only that their youngest daughters' responses fall short of the lavish praise which their older daughters heap on them. While we have no evidence to suggest whether or not Shakespeare was familiar with the story of *The Goose Girl at the Well,* his play and the folk tale certainly reflect some of the same timeless themes of the love between parent and child, the difficulty of expressing that love, and the danger of mistaking flattery for love and honest speech for dislike; and perhaps it is the mythical nature of the story that appealed to Shakespeare and that has helped the play to endure for so long and to appeal to so many.

FROM JACOB AND WILHELM GRIMM, *THE GOOSE GIRL AT THE WELL,* IN *GRIMM'S HOUSEHOLD TALES,* TRANS. MARGARET HUNT

(London and New York: G. Bell and Sons, 1892)

When the Queen was alone, she began to weep bitterly, and said, "Of what use to me are the splendours and honours with which I am surrounded; every morning I awake in pain and sorrow. I had three daughters, the youngest of whom was so beautiful that the whole world looked on her as a wonder. She was as white as snow, as rosy as apple-blossom, and her hair as radiant as sunbeams. When she cried, not tears fell from her eyes, but pearls and jewels only. When she was fifteen years old, the King summoned all three sisters to come before his throne. You should have seen how all the people gazed when the youngest entered, it was just as if the sun were rising! Then the King spoke, 'My daughters, I know not when my last day may arrive; I will to-day decide what each shall receive at my death. You all love me, but the one of you who loves me best, shall fare the best.' Each of them said she loved him best. 'Can you not express to me,' said the King, 'how much you do love me, and thus I shall see what you mean?' The eldest spoke. 'I love my father as dearly as the sweetest sugar.' The second, 'I love my father as dearly as my prettiest dress.' But the youngest was silent. Then the father said, 'And thou, my dearest child, how much dost thou love me?' 'I do not know, and can compare my love with nothing.' But her father insisted that she should name something. So she said at last, 'The best food does not please me without salt, therefore I love my father like salt.' When the King heard that, he fell into a passion, and said, 'If thou lovest me like salt, thy love shall also be repaid thee with salt.' Then he divided the kingdom between the two elder, but caused a sack of salt to be bound on the back of the youngest, and two servants had to lead her forth into the wild forest. We all begged and prayed for her,' said the Queen, 'but the King's anger was not to be appeased. How she cried when she had to leave us! The whole road was strewn with the pearls which flowed from her eyes. The King soon afterwards repented of his great severity, and had the whole forest searched for the poor child, but no one could find her." (286–7)

LITERATURE REVISED

Not only did the story of King Lear exist in the chronicles of English history, but it had also been told in various works of literature before Shakespeare revised it. Readers in the late sixteenth century might have encountered the story in Edmund Spenser's *The Faerie Queene,* in which one of the characters reads the history of King Lear and his daughters in a chronicle of English history, or they might have read *A Mirror for Magistrates,* a collection of moral poems about famous kings, queens, and nobles, in which the story is told from the dead Cordelia's point of view as a lesson about the sin of suicide. Shakespeare's original audience might even have seen another play about King Lear. The anonymous play, *The True Chronicle History of King Leir and His Three Daughters, Gonorill, Ragan, and Cordella* had been performed in London as early as 1594. Like most of the histories and poems, *King Leir* focuses a great deal of attention of the fact that the king did not have a son. Although the anonymous play does suggest that the king was at fault for using the love test in an attempt to trick his youngest daughter into marrying the suitor of his choice, it also implies that the king's tragedy could have been averted if he had had a male heir. In the opening lines of the play the king mourns the recent death of his wife and his lack of a son:

> A son we want for to succeed our crown,
> And course of time hath cancelled the date
> Of further issue from our withered loins. (1.1.19–21)

In the following excerpt, taken from the first scene, the king discusses this predicament with some noblemen, who join him in mourning the lack of a clear heir, or an "heir indubitate" (1.1.42), and suggest that to remedy this situation he should marry his daughters off to the kings of nearby countries so that there will be peace between the kingdoms. Leir then presents his plan to trick his youngest daughter into marrying the king of Brittany. The lack of a son thus becomes the cause not only of the division of the kingdom between Leir's three daughters but also, indirectly, of the love test which is the first of the king's tragic mistakes.

FROM *THE TRUE CHRONICLE HISTORY OF KING LEIR AND HIS THREE DAUGHTERS, GONORILL, RAGAN AND CORDELLA* (C 1594), ED. A. F. HOPKINSON

(London, 1895)

Nobleman: My gracious lord, I heartily do wish
That God had lent you an heir indubitate,
Which might have set upon your royal throne,
When fates should loose the prison of your life,
By whose succession all this doubt might cease,
And as by you, by him we might have peace:
But after-wishes ever come too late,
And nothing can revoke the course of fate.
Wherefore, my liege, my censure deems it best,
To match them with some of your neighbor kings,
Bord'ring within the bounds of Albion,
By whose united friendship, this our state
May be protected 'gainst all foreign hate.

Leir: Herein, my lords, your wishes sort with mine,
And mine, I hope, do sort with heavenly powers;
For at this instant two near neighboring kings,
Of Cornwall and of Cambria, motion love
To my two daughters Gonorill and Ragan.
My youngest daughter, fair Cordella, vows
No liking to a monarch, unless love allows.
She is solicited by divers peers,
But none of them her partial fancy hears;
Yet if my policy may her beguile,
I'll match her to some king within this isle;
And so establish such a perfect peace,
As fortune's force shall ne'er prevail to cease.

Perillus: Of us and ours, your gracious care, my lord,
Deserves an everlasting memory,
To be enrolled in chronicles of fame,
By never-dying perpetuity;
Yet to become so provident a prince,
Lose not the title of a loving father:
Do not force love where fancy cannot dwell,
Lest streams being stopped, above the banks do swell.

Leir: I am resolved and even now my mind
Doth meditate a sudden stratagem,
To try which of my daughters loves me best;
Which till I know I cannot be in rest.

This granted, when they jointly shall contend,
Each to exceed the other in their love,
Then at the vantage will I take Cordella,
Even as she doth protest she loves me best,
I'll say—'Then, daughter, grant me one request,
To show thou lov'st me as thy sisters do,
Accept a husband whom myself will woo.'
This said, she cannot well deny my suit,
Although—poor soul!—her senses will be mute;
Then will I triumph in my policy
And match her with a king of Brittany. (1.1.41–89)

Shakespeare, of course, will eliminate this focus on the dangers of having only daughters and will do this in part by adding the subplot of Gloucester and his sons, borrowed from Sir Philip Sidney's *Arcadia,* which clearly shows that the source of the tragedy lies in fathers misjudging their children, not in the gender of the children. In book two of Sidney's *Arcadia* the heroes of the story see a blind, old man wandering though a storm, led by his loyal son. They question the men and learn how the father was deceived by his illegitimate son who robbed him of his kingdom and put out his eyes. Like Gloucester, the blind king now wants to end his life. In the following excerpt the blind king, having just related how he planned the murder of his loyal son after being deceived by his illegitimate and treacherous son, explains how his legitimate son forgave him and took care of him in his blindness. From this excerpt it is clear that the blind king is not only the source of Gloucester, but also has many similarities to Lear. Both mistakenly trust the wrong children; both are left with "nothing but the name of a king," and both end up wandering in a storm. Incorporating this character and his story into *King Lear* thus provides a mirror image of the main plot.

FROM SIR PHILIP SIDNEY, *THE COUNTESS OF PEMBROKE'S ARCADIA* (1590), ED. OSKAR SOMMER

(London, 1891)

But those thieves (better natured to my son than myself) spared his life, letting him go, to learn to live poorly, which he did, giving himself to be a private soldier, in a country hereby. But as he was ready to be greatly advanced for some noble pieces of service which he did, he heard news of me, who (drunk in my affection to that unlawful and unnatural son of mine) suffered myself so to be governed by him that all favors and punishments passed by him, all offices, and places of importance, distributed to his favourites; so that, ere I was aware, I had left myself nothing but the name of a king, which he shortly weary of too, with many indignities (if anything may be called an indignity, which was laid upon me) threw me out of my seat, and put out my eyes; and then (proud in his tyranny) let me go, neither imprisoning, nor killing me, but rather delighting to make me feel my misery; misery indeed, if ever there were any; full of wretchedness, fuller of disgrace, and fullest of guiltiness. And as he came to the crown by so unjust means, as unjustly he kept it, by force of stranger soldiers in *Cittadels*, the nests of tyranny, & murderers of liberty; disarming all his own countrymen, that no man durst show himself a well-willer of mine. To say the truth (I think) few of them being so (considering my cruel folly to my good son, and foolish kindness to my unkind bastard). But if there were any who fell to pity of so great a fall, and had yet any sparks of unstained duty left in them towards me, yet durst they not show it, scarcely with giving me alms at their doors; which yet was the only sustenance of my distressed life, nobody daring to show so much charity, as to lend me a hand to guide my dark steps. Till this son of mine (God knows, worthy of a more virtuous and more fortunate father) forgetting my abominable wrongs, not recking danger, & neglecting the present good way he was in doing himself good, came hither to do this kind office you see him perform towards me. (143–5)

TRAGEDY

King Lear is one of Shakespeare's great tragedies. But what exactly is a tragedy? Most students know that a tragedy is sad and deals with serious issues while a comedy is happy and may deal with lighter themes, and that a tragedy ends in death while a comedy ends in marriage. *King Lear* certainly deals with serious issues and ends in the deaths of many of the main characters, but it can also be labeled a tragedy because it follows in the literary traditions of tragedies which date back to ancient Greece.

ARISTOTLE

The Greek philosopher Aristotle's definitions of tragedy and the tragic hero have been influential since he set them down in *The Poetics* (c. 330 B.C.). These definitions were considered especially important during the Renaissance, when many writers modeled their works on the works of ancient Greece and Rome. According to Aristotle, tragedies had to follow the descent of a central character, the tragic hero, from a high and noble position to a low one. The tragic hero had to possess some tragic flaw which caused his fall from fortune, or reversal of fortune, and at some point he had to realize that his own errors had caused his reversal of fortune, though it would then be too late for him to correct his mistakes. Finally, Aristotle noted that the fall of the hero should arouse pity and fear in the audience because they will sympathize with the character and fear a similar fate. In the following excerpt, Aristotle discusses the character of the tragic hero and explains why the hero must be an essentially good, but flawed, man.

FROM ARISTOTLE, *THE POETICS* (C. 330 B.C.), IN
ARISTOTLE'S THEORY OF POETRY AND FINE ART, TRANS.
S. H. BUTCHER

(London: Macmillan, 1907)

A perfect tragedy should . . . be arranged not on the simple but on the complex plan. It should, moreover, imitate actions which excite pity and fear, this being the distinctive mark of tragic imitation. It follows plainly, in the first place, that the change of fortune presented must not be the spectacle of a virtuous man brought from prosperity to adversity: for this moves neither pity nor fear; it merely shocks us. Nor, again, that of a bad man passing from adversity to prosperity: for nothing can be more alien to the spirit of tragedy; it possesses no single tragic quality; it neither satisfies the moral sense nor calls forth pity or fear. Nor, again, should the downfall of the utter villain be exhibited. A plot of this kind would, doubtless, satisfy the moral sense, but it would inspire neither pity nor fear; for pity is aroused by unmerited misfortune, fear by the misfortune of a man like ourselves. Such an event, therefore, will be neither pitiful nor terrible. There remains, then, the character between these two extremes—that of a man who is not eminently good and just, yet whose misfortune is brought about not by vice or depravity, but by some error or frailty. He must be one who is highly renowned and prosperous,—a personage like Oedipus, Thyestes, or other illustrious men of such families.

A well constructed plot should, therefore, be single in its issue, rather than double as some maintain. The change of fortune should be not from bad to good, but reversely, from good to bad. It should come about as the result not of vice, but of some great error or frailty, in a character either such as we have described, or better rather than worse. (45, 47)

Thus, if we are to consider King Lear a tragic hero in the tradition of Aristotle, we must see him as a basically good king who nevertheless possesses some flaws, which bring about his downfall. He cannot be wholly good, or his fall will seem undeserved, but he cannot be entirely evil or the audience will feel no regret at his downfall. If we look from the viewpoint of Goneril and Regan, of course, we might find that Lear is far too flawed to be a tragic hero. We might feel, as they do, that "he hath ever but slenderly known himself" and that "the infirmity of his age" has weakened his judgment still further (1.2.291–2). But while Lear makes, especially in the early scenes of the play, numerous terrible errors in judgment, the love of Cordelia and the loyalty of Kent lead us to believe that he has been both a good father and a good king in the past. And while his errors in judgment may result, as his elder daughters suggest, from his old age and senility, he is clearly still reasonable enough to recognize the results of his actions and the error of his ways. In the final scenes of the play it is clear that he has recognized his mistakes and regrets his treatment of Cordelia.

But while Lear may be a tragic hero according to Aristotle's definition, other elements of *King Lear* do not conform to what Aristotle would consider "a perfect tragedy." As noted in the excerpt above, Aristotle felt that tragedies should have only one plot, not a double plot like that of *King Lear*. Aristotle also defined the types of plots that he felt were most likely to evoke pity and fear. In the following excerpt he explains the desirable qualities of a tragic plot.

Let us then determine what are the circumstances which strike us as terrible or pitiful.

Actions capable of this effect must happen between persons who are either friends or enemies or indifferent to one another. If an enemy kills an enemy, there is nothing to excite pity either in the act or the intention,—except so far as the suffering in itself is pitiful. So again with indifferent persons. But when the tragic incident occurs between those who are near or dear to one another— if, for example, a brother kills, or intends to kill, a brother, a son his father, a mother her son, a son his mother, or any other deed of the kind is done—these are the situations to be looked for by the poet. He may not indeed destroy the framework of the received legends—the fact, for instance, that Clytemnestra was slain by Orestes and Eriphyle by Alcmaeon—but he ought to show invention of his own, and skillfully handle the traditional material. (49, 51)

In the story of King Lear and his daughters, Shakespeare clearly found a story in which the "tragic incident occurs between those who are near or dear to one another." He did, however, deviate from Aristotelian form by changing the "framework of the received legends." He did not relate the story as it had been told in the historical chronicles, but instead made the story even more tragic by adding the deaths of Lear and Cordelia at the end. While this might be seen as an example of Shakespeare's "invention" and skillful handling of the story, it is also evidence that Shakespeare was both working within the Aristotelian tradition of tragedy and adapting traditional forms to suit his own artistic vision.

TATE AND JOHNSON

Though *King Lear* is today generally regarded as an excellent example of Shakespearean tragedy, it has not always been so well received. In the two centuries after Shakespeare wrote this play, some readers simply found the ending too tragic. Rather than moving them to pity and fear, it moved them to despair. In 1681, a playwright named Nahum Tate rewrote the play, making several changes that will be discussed in more detail in chapter five, including a new and happy ending in which Cordelia and Edgar fall in love and inherit the kingdom which has been restored to Lear. Many people, it appears, preferred this happy ending to Shakespeare's tragic one, and in the eighteenth century Samuel Johnson, a well-respected writer and perhaps the best Shakespearean critic of his day, wrote an analysis of *King Lear* in which he praised the artistry of the play and defended the use of the double plot, but criticized the pessimistic ending. His mention of a contrary opinion, expressed in *The Spectator,* a contemporary periodical, however, makes it evident that even in the eighteenth century some readers preferred Shakespeare's tragic ending to Tate's happy one.

FROM SAMUEL JOHNSON, AFTERWORD TO *KING LEAR* (1765), IN *JOHNSON ON SHAKESPEARE,* ED. WALTER RALEIGH

(London: Oxford University Press, 1929)

The Tragedy of *Lear* is deservedly celebrated among the dramas of *Shakespeare.* There is perhaps no play which keeps the attention so strongly fixed; which so much agitates our passions and interests our curiosity. The artful involutions of distinct interests, the striking opposition of contrary characters, the sudden changes of fortune, and the quick succession of events, fill the mind with a perpetual tumult of indignation, pity, and hope. There is no scene which does not contribute to the aggravation of the distress or conduct of the action, and scarce a line which does not conduce to the progress of the scene. So powerful is the current of the poet's imagination, that the mind, which once ventures within it, is hurried irresistibly along. . . .

The injury done by *Edmund* to the simplicity of the action is abundantly recompensed by the addition of variety, by the art with which he is made to co-operate with the chief design, and the opportunity which he gives the poet of combining perfidy with perfidy, and connecting the wicked son with the wicked daughters, to impress this important moral, that villainy is never at a stop, that crimes lead to crimes, and at last terminate in ruin.

But though this moral be incidentally enforced, Shakespeare has suffered the virtue of *Cordelia* to perish in a just cause, contrary to the natural ideas of justice, to the hope of the reader, and what is yet more strange, to the faith of chronicles. Yet this conduct is justified by the Spectator, who blames *Tate* for giving *Cordelia* success and happiness in his alteration, and declares that, in his opinion, *the tragedy has lost half its beauty*. . . . A play in which the wicked prosper, and the virtuous miscarry, may doubtless be good, because it is a just representation of the common events of human life: but since all reasonable beings naturally love justice, I cannot easily be persuaded, that the observation of justice makes a play worse; or, that if other excellencies are equal, the audience will not always rise better pleased from the final triumph of persecuted virtue.

In the present case the public has decided. *Cordelia,* from the time of *Tate,* has always retired with victory and felicity. And, if my sensations could add anything to the general suffrage, I might relate, that I was many years ago so shocked by *Cordelia*'s death, that I know not whether I ever endured to read again the last scenes of the play till I undertook to revise them as an editor. (159–62)

THE TEXTS OF *KING LEAR*

What is a Shakespearean text? Shakespeare wrote his plays for performance, not for publication. Although his plays were very popular during his lifetime, only about half of them were published before his death, and he does not appear to have been involved in the publication process of those plays. Theater, furthermore, is a collaborative art form. The playwright writes the original text, but changes may later be made by directors and actors, or by the playwright himself. In Shakespeare's day, once the playwright had written the play, the text became the property of the theatrical company for which he had written it, and the company might later choose to sell the text to a publisher to supplement the company's income. Additional changes might then be made to the text during the printing process, which, in the seventeenth century was still relatively new and subject to error. Because of all of these factors, there is often more than one existing version of a single Shakespeare play, and we cannot always be certain which is the version Shakespeare would have preferred. The differences between two texts may represent revisions that Shakespeare made, revisions made by actors, directors, or publishers, or errors accidentally introduced along the way. Thus, any time we read or see a Shakespeare play, we are seeing a series of choices made by an editor or director.

In the case of *King Lear* there are two texts. One was included in the *Folio Shakespeare,* the first collected edition of Shakespeare's works, which was printed in 1623, seven years after Shakespeare's death. The other was a quarto text printed in 1608. (*Quarto* and *folio* refer to the bookmaking format and the number of times a large sheet of paper was folded to make the pages of the book. For folios, the large sheets of paper used in book printing were folded once, creating two leaves, or four pages, since each leaf would be printed on the front and back. The pages would measure about 9 by 14 inches. For quartos the large sheet of paper was folded twice, producing four leaves—hence the term quarto—or eight pages, which would measure about 7 by 9 inches, or roughly the size of the book you are now reading. Folios were larger and more expensive than quartos.)

There are substantial differences between the two texts. The quarto, titled *The History of King Lear,* contains about 300 lines that are not printed in the folio. The folio, titled *The Tragedy of King Lear,* contains about 100 lines that are not printed in the quarto, and there are numerous smaller differences. Scholars generally believe that these two versions of the play represent an early version and a later revision by Shakespeare, and it is interesting for scholars to compare the two versions and speculate on the reasons for the changes. But the presence of two texts need not confuse or frustrate the general reader of Shakespeare. In the eighteenth century a conflated text, or a text which combined the folio and the quarto, was created, and this has been the text that readers and playgoers have generally encountered since then.

PATTERNS IN THE PLAY

One fruitful way to analyze the play is to look for patterns. Recurring words, phrases, character types, or images can point to some of the important themes and ideas of the play. Once we recognize the existence of a certain pattern, we can question why it is there, what role it is playing, what it contributes to our experience of the play, and what it means when that pattern is broken.

Language

Although Shakespeare's language is considered early modern English, it may at first be difficult for modern readers to understand. Much of this confusion can be alleviated by seeing the plays performed, either on stage or in film. Many students of Shakespeare find that it is much easier for them to follow the action of the plays, laugh at the humor of the comedies, and feel the pain of the tragedies when they see the plays performed. Nevertheless, this does not mean that the plays should not be read or that the language should not be studied. Shakespeare borrowed the plots of most of his plays, and it is largely his choice of language that sets his plays apart from their source texts and from later revisions and adaptations. Though challenging at first, Shakespeare's language is a great source of pleasure for many readers, and analyzing it can lead to a greater understanding of the language itself and of the ideas it helps to convey.

In *King Lear,* language is particularly important because the untrustworthiness of language is an important theme in the play. The play begins with Lear's foolish request that his daughters demonstrate their love for him through language. Even the lying Goneril's claim that she loves him "more than words can wield the matter" and that her love for him "makes breath poor, and speech unable," demonstrates the problem with this request (1.1.53, 58). Language can lie. Vows and promises of love can be broken. In contrast to her sisters' lies and flattery, Cordelia responds with a truthful "nothing" (1.1.86). She knows that there is nothing she can say to win at this game of flattery, and she recognizes that her words cannot adequately express her love since she "cannot heave / [her] heart into [her] mouth" (1.1.90–1), but Lear misunderstands her words and hears in her "nothing" only emptiness and a lack of love. The word *nothing* will echo throughout the play. Edmund will claim that the forged letter with which he wants to incriminate his brother is "nothing" (1.2.31); he will then tell Edgar that he has only conveyed the danger Edgar is in "faintly, nothing like the image and horror of it" (1.4.160–1). And when Edgar gives up his identity and disguises himself as Poor Tom, he will declare, "Edgar I nothing am" (2.3.21). Outside of Goneril's castle the Fool will teasingly remind Lear that he has nothing left of his kingdom, and the King's reply that "nothing can be made out of nothing" will sadly echo his advice to Cordelia: "Nothing will come of nothing, speak again" (1.4.114;1.1.89). Out in the storm, the mad Lear will endure the winds which "make nothing of" his white hair (3.1.9); he will vow to be "the pattern of all patience" and "say nothing" (3.2.36). Upon seeing Poor Tom he will ask the beggar "couldst thou save nothing?" (3.4.62), and when he is told that Tom's misery is not the result of treacherous daughters he will respond, "nothing could have subdued nature / To such lowness but his unkind daughters" (3.4.67–8).

The frequent repetition of the word serves two purposes. It emphasizes the desolation of the kingdom. Lear has nothing left, and as a result of his mistakes the kingdom is being reduced to nothing. At the same time, the repetition of the word reminds us that what appears to be nothing may in fact be of greater value than what appears to be everything. Goneril and Regan claimed to love their father above all else, but their lies amounted to nothing. Cordelia's answer seemed like nothing, but in fact her love proves to be by far the strongest, continuing even after her father has nothing to offer her and has, indeed, already disowned her. Only after having lost everything does Lear realize the emptiness of his eldest daughters' words: "They told me I was everything. 'Tis a lie, I am not ague-proof" (4.6.102–3). Only after losing everything can he recognize his own faults and vulnerabilities, and only then can he appreciate the value of Cordelia's honest reply.

Theatrical Conventions

Although drama is, as Aristotle noted, an imitation of life, it is an imitation full of its own conventions, or devices, which the audience knows to be false, but which it accepts as real for the duration of the play. An audience, for example, suspends disbelief and accepts the fact that Kent could disguise himself so effectively that he would not be recognized by the king who had recently banished him and whom he had served closely and loyally for years. The speech of characters in a play is also governed by theatrical conventions. Though much of the play is made up of dialogue between two or more characters, single characters may also speak asides or soliloquies. An aside is a brief comment made by one character, which is not heard by the other characters on the stage. A soliloquy is a speech delivered by one character while that character is alone on stage. Both asides and soliloquies are used to inform the audience of the true feelings or intentions of the character. Thus, even a character like Edmund, who lies to the other characters in the play, can be assumed to be telling the truth when he speaks his soliloquy at the beginning of act one, scene two. It is, therefore, crucial to pay attention to theatrical conventions since they can provide clues to the true meaning of the characters' actions and speech.

Characters

Patterns can also be detected in characters. We may, for instance, see many examples of a particular type of character. While out on the heath in the storm, the Fool declares, "This cold night will turn us all to fools and madmen" (3.4.75), and indeed, there do seem to be many fools and madmen in the play. There are also many treacherous children, and they highlight the loyalty and goodness of those children and servants who do not betray their fathers or masters. The presence of many similar characters suggests a pattern that merits further investigation.

Fools

While talking with Lear and the disguised Kent in front of Goneril's castle, the Fool notes that he is far from being the only fool in the Kingdom. In fact, he complains that all the other fools are infringing on his business: "no, faith, lords and great men will not let me; if I had a monopoly out, they would have part on 't: and ladies too, they will not let me have all fool to myself; they'll be snatching" (1.4.133–5). Indeed, we see much foolish behavior in the play, and many people are called fools. The Fool calls Lear a fool, observing that he has given away all his other titles, but "that thou wast born with" (1.4.130–1). Lear tells Gloucester, "When we are born, we cry that we are come / To this great stage of fools" (4.6.177), and when mourning the death of Cordelia he says, "my poor fool is hanged!" (5.3.304). All of this may lead us to question exactly what it means to be a fool in this play. Lear has certainly been foolish in giving away his kingdom and trusting his least trustworthy children, but in what sense is Cordelia a fool? And how is the Fool a fool, since he often seems to be the least foolish of all, able as he is to speak honestly to Lear without fear of banishment? It is helpful to know that Shakespeare wrote two different sorts of roles for fools in his plays, depending in part on the actor who was to play them. In his early plays, when the fool was played by Will Kemp, the parts tended to be light and humorous, but in 1599 Will Kemp left Shakespeare's company and was replaced by Robert Armin, and Shakespeare's fools became much wiser and more serious. In spite of being professional fools, those responsible for providing the court with entertainment and amusement, they are often wise and reflective, and seemingly the most reasonable characters in the play. Lear's fool falls into this category. He functions as a voice of reason for Lear, reminding him of his mistakes and advising him. He also takes the place of Lear's children when his daughters have either betrayed him or been betrayed by him. After Goneril and Regan have cast Lear out in the storm, the Fool follows him and "labors to out-jest / His heart-struck injuries" (3.2.16–7), and when Lear is raging in the storm, unable to think of his own physical discomfort because of his mental anguish, he is still able to feel concern for the Fool: "Poor fool and knave, I have one part in my heart / That's sorry yet for thee" (3.2.70–1). It may then be surprising for readers to realize that this important character actually disappears from the play after act three, scene six. As Kent is preparing to take Lear to Dover, he instructs the fool, "Come, help to bear thy master: Thou must not stay behind (3.6.94–5), but this is the last mention ever made of the Fool in the play. Is Lear so far gone into madness that he can no longer benefit from the voice of reason? Does he now feel so far separated from humanity that he no longer has even "one part" of his heart left with which to feel concern for the Fool? Has Lear become his own fool, and if so, in what sense? Or does the Fool disappear because his role will soon be taken over by Cordelia, the poor fool to be hanged?

Madmen

If there are many fools in the play, there are also several madmen. Goneril and Regan suspect Lear of being senile at the beginning of the play, and they note that he "hath ever but slenderly known himself" (1.2.290). But even if

Kate Eastwood Norris plays Fool and Craig Wallace the title role in the 2003–2004 *King Lear* at Shenandoah Shakespeare's Blackfriars Playhouse in Staunton, Virginia. Photo by Michael Bailey. Courtesy of Shenandoah Shakespeare.

we do not believe him to be senile or demented at the beginning of the play, we certainly see him pushed towards madness over the course of the play. He fights valiantly against it, fervently praying "O, let me not be mad, not mad, sweet heaven! / Keep me in temper; I would not be mad!" (1.5.38–9), but towards the end of the play it is doubtful whether he knows himself even slenderly. The physicians Cordelia provides bring some temporary relief, but in the final scene his sorrows again seem too much for him to endure, and it is unclear whether he dies with the delusional belief that Cordelia is still alive, or whether the realization that she is dead because of his mistakes is the blow that finally kills him. Lear's madness, of course, is also mirrored in the feigned madness of Edgar (as Poor Tom) and in the suicidal despair of Gloucester. The existence of these three different types of "madmen" along with the insane cruelty of other characters forces us to question what madness is, how the different forms of madness shown in the play are related, and why one person goes mad while another manages to endure and to stay sane.

Fathers and Children

If Lear's madness is mirrored by Gloucester's despair, Lear's mistakes as a father are also reflected in Gloucester's misjudgment of his sons. Likewise, the treachery of Goneril and Regan is mirrored in Edmund's betrayal of his father and brother. These characters stand in sharp contrast to Cordelia and Edgar, who remain loyal and devoted to their fathers even when their fathers have mistreated or betrayed them. The inclusion of the Gloucester subplot, as already noted, prevents the play from being a warning about the dangers of not having male children. The fact that several nonrelatives, Kent, the Fool, and the nameless servant of Cornwall who dies defending Gloucester's eyes, actually prove to be more loyal and devoted than the children of Lear and Gloucester also raises the question of what really binds people together. Although Cordelia says that she loves her father "according to [her] bond," that is, as a daughter should love her father, the bonds of family in this play often prove weaker than the bonds of loyal service and friendship.

Other Motifs

In addition to patterns of language and character, we may find other recurrent motifs that point to central themes in the play. For example, when Lear encounters Poor Tom wandering naked in the storm he asks:

> Is man no more than this? Consider him well. Thou owest the worm no silk, the beast no hide, the sheep no wool, the cat no perfume. Ha! Here's three on's are sophisticated! Thou art the thing itself: unaccommodated man is no more but such a poor, bare, forked animal as thou art. (3.4.95–100)

The question of what separates humans from animals will run throughout the play. Before being cast out in the storm Lear tries to explain to Goneril and Regan that "man's life's as cheap as beast's" if that man has only the bare necessities, but in the storm he sees a man who even seems to lack the most basic necessities, and who has indeed been reduced to a sort of beast, "a poor, bare, forked animal" (2.4.262; 3.4.99–100). Even in the final, tragic scene, Lear still seems to be questioning what separates humans from animals when he grieves over Cordelia's dead body and asks "Why should a dog, a horse, a rat, have life, / And thou no breath at all?" (5.3.305–6). Ultimately the play seems to suggest that what keeps us from becoming beasts is our ability to preserve noble, decent human values even in the face of terrible cruelty and desolation. Edgar, Kent, and Cordelia rise above mere animal nature, and behave nobly even when they are mistreated, whereas Regan, Goneril, and Edmund become monstrous beasts, even killing and maiming members of their own families.

THEMES

Themes are the dominant or central ideas of a piece of literature. Having detected some of the patterns in *King Lear,* we can determine some of the themes. It is not enough, however, to merely identify the patterns in the play. Noting that there are many fools in the play, for example, is only the first step in analysis. We next need to consider what the play is saying about fools, or what the presence of all those fools signifies. We might, therefore, say that one theme in *King Lear* is that the wisest people are those who recognize their own folly. Being a complex work of literature, *King Lear* will, of course, have many themes. There will, furthermore, be many ways to interpret different motifs, and while those interpretations must be supported by evidence in the play, there is more than one "right" interpretation. We analyze a work of literature in order to understand its meaning, themes, and ideas, but a complex work like *King Lear* will offer more than one simple meaning.

QUESTIONS FOR WRITTEN AND ORAL DISCUSSION

1. According to Aristotle, a tragic hero has to have a tragic flaw, a weakness that brings about his tragic reversal of fortune. For example, tragic heroes are often overly proud, believing that they can control their own fates. Read act 1, scene 1 of *King Lear,* making a list of Lear's mistakes and errors in judgment. Compare your list with the lists of other students. Based on this evidence, what is Lear's tragic flaw?

2. Tragedies, according to Aristotle, should inspire their audience with fear and pity. Does *King Lear* make you feel fear and pity? What scenes of the play provoke these feelings? Do you feel one emotion more than the other?

3. Aristotle asserts that tragedies should not have a double plot, but one of Shakespeare's innovations was to combine the Lear plot and the Gloucester plot. Why do you think he might have added the second plot? Does the second plot reinforce the themes of the first plot? How so? Give specific examples. In your opinion, does the

second plot distract the reader or viewer from the force of the first plot, or do they complement each other?

4. One of Shakespeare's most surprising changes to the legend of King Lear was to end the play with the deaths of both Lear and Cordelia. Read the excerpt of Holinshed's *Chronicles* and the last scene of *King Lear*. Which ending do you prefer? Why do you think Shakespeare might have made this change? Prepare to defend your answer in a class debate.

5. Samuel Johnson criticized Shakespeare's ending of the play because, while he acknowledged that it might represent the common triumph of evil over good, it deviated from historical record and violated the ideas of justice. Do you think it is more important for a play to end justly, for a play to represent the tragic situations one might encounter in real life, or for a play to represent historical fact? Prepare to debate your ideas with the class.

6. Read the letters from the Sir Bryan Annesley case. Using those letters as your models, write letters from the point of view of two of the following characters: Cordelia, Regan, Goneril, Albany, Cornwall, the Fool, and Kent. In your letter, argue whether or not you think King Lear should be deprived of his kingdom and declared insane. Use evidence from the play to support your argument. Be prepared to read your letters to the class.

7. How does the Lear depicted in Geoffrey of Monmouth's *History* differ from Shakespeare's Lear? Compare especially Lear's speech at the end of the excerpt of Geoffrey's *History* and the speeches of Shakespeare's Lear in the storm scenes (3.2, 3.4, and 3.6). Which Lear do you prefer? Which makes a better tragic hero?

8. Aristotle asserts that a tragic hero should recognize that his own mistakes brought about his tragic end. While Lear clearly recognizes that he has trusted the wrong daughters, it is unclear whether, in the final scene of the play, he truly understands that Cordelia is dead as a result of his errors in judgment. Read the final scene, beginning with Lear's entrance with Cordelia in his arms (5.3.256). Do you think he realizes that she is dead, or does he die deluding himself that she is still alive? What evidence do you see to support your interpretation? Why might Shakespeare have left the ending ambiguous?

9. Shakespeare added the character of the Fool to *King Lear*. None of the earlier versions of the story had included such a character. Why might Shakespeare have added him? What does his character add to the play? Why does he disappear after act three?

10. Directors of *King Lear* have handled the disappearance of the Fool in a variety of different ways. Some have had him stay behind in the hovel when Kent carries Lear off to Dover. Some have shown him wandering off into the storm. Others have simply let him drop from the script without explanation, and still others have shown him being captured by soldiers of Goneril and Regan. Imagine that you are directing *King Lear*. How would you stage the Fool's disappearance? Get together with some of your classmates and prepare to act out the end of act three, scene six, for the class. Be prepared to explain your reasons for staging the scene in the manner you have chosen.

11. We have examined the repetition of the word *nothing* throughout the play. Other words which are frequently repeated include *mad, fool, endure, burst, patience, cruel,* and *division.* Choose one of these words and trace it (or forms of it) throughout the play. You will probably want to use a concordance or the find-command in an internet edition of *King Lear* to help you. What pattern do you see? What conclusions can you draw about this pattern? What themes can you arrive at based on your interpretation of this pattern?

12. The Fool complains that he cannot keep a monopoly on foolishness because so many other people insist on behaving in a foolish manner. Who is the biggest or the best fool in the play? Your answer, of course, will depend on how you define fool. Do you mean someone who behaves in an absurd manner, someone who makes stupid mistakes, or someone who wisely points out the folly of others? Use evidence from the text to support your answer.

13. Lear, Gloucester, and Poor Tom (Edgar) are the three clearest examples of madness in the play. What are the differences between these three characters and their mental states? Why are we given these three different types of madness? What does the presence of these three characters tell you about madness in the play?

14. Do a character study of one character in *King Lear.* Look carefully at the character's language and actions. Pay special attention to any soliloquies and asides, and to discrepancies between what the character says to the audience and what he or she says to other characters in the play. What can you learn about the character from a careful analysis of language and actions? Present your findings to the class.

15. A foil is a character that defines another character by contrast. Originally the term referred to a sheet of metal placed under a jewel to enhance its brilliance. Which of the characters in *King Lear* are foils for each other? Keep in mind that in order to be foils the characters must have some similarities, but some notable differences. Choose one such pair of characters and explain to the class how one character sets off the attributes of the other.

SUGGESTED READINGS

Boswell-Stone, W. G., ed. *Shakespeare's Holinshed: The Chronicle and the Historical Plays Compared.* Vol. 3. London: Chatto & Windus, 1907.

Bullough, Geoffrey, ed. *Narrative and Dramatic Sources of Shakespeare.* Vol. 7. London: Routledge, 1973.

Greenblatt, Stephen. Critical Introduction to *King Lear. The Norton Shakespeare.* Ed. Greenblatt, et al. New York: Norton, 1997.

McDonald, Russ, ed. *The Bedford Companion to Shakespeare: An Introduction with Documents.* Boston: Bedford, 1996.

Weis, René. Critical Introduction. *King Lear: A Parallel Text Edition.* London: Longman, 1993.

2

"That way madness lies": Insanity in Shakespeare's Time

In the midst of the storm, sitting in a hovel with Edgar, Lear, and Kent, the fool complains that "this cold night will turn us all to fools and madmen" (3.4.75), and indeed there seem to be an inordinate number of madmen in the play. Lear, possibly senile at the beginning of the play, is driven further and further into madness by the betrayal of his daughters and the loss of his kingdom. Gloucester, after his blinding, wanders in despair and attempts suicide, and Edgar, in order to escape the wrath of his father, pretends to be a mad beggar released from Bedlam, the oldest insane asylum in England. These characters and their actions may be difficult for modern students of Shakespeare to understand if they do not know something about how madness was perceived and treated in Shakespeare's day. This chapter will present documents illustrating the perceptions and treatment of madness in the early modern period. The spelling and punctuation of the documents included in this chapter have been modernized where necessary for the sake of clarity.

CAUSES OF MADNESS

Modern psychologists and psychiatrists offer many explanations of the causes of mental disorders. Some argue that the diseases of the mind are caused by physical disorders, such as an imbalance of hormones or chemicals. Others look to the environment in which the person suffering from a mental disorder now lives, or the environment in which the patient was raised. Many suggest some combination of these theories. Likewise, in the early modern pe-

Laurence Olivier plays the mad King Lear in director Michael Elliot's 1984 televised version of *King Lear*. Reprinted with permission of Photofest.

riod, there were many different theories about the causes of madness, and often those theories were combined. A physician might well believe that madness was sometimes caused by an imbalance of humors or bodily fluids and at other times caused by the order of the stars or the heavens, or he might believe that the stars influenced the humors. This chapter will provide an introduction to some of the more commonly held beliefs about the causes of madness in Shakespeare's day.

The Four Humors

Probably the most widely accepted theory of the causes of mental illness in Shakespeare's day was humoral theory. This theory was derived from the ideas of ancient Greek philosophers who thought that the world and all the matter in it were made up of four basic elements: earth, water, air, and fire. The Roman physician Galen, in the second century A.D., expanded on these theories, and hence the medical theories that resulted are often known as Galenic medicine. According to Galenic medicine, the four elements occur in the human body in the form of four liquids, or humors: blood, phlegm, choler (also known as yellow bile), and melancholy (also known as black bile). These elements and their corresponding humors were characterized according to whether they were hot or cold, dry or moist. Air and blood were hot and moist. Water and phlegm were cold and moist. Fire and choler were hot and dry. Earth and black bile were cold and dry. The dominance of one humor could affect the personality. A choleric person, or a person with too much choler, would be easily irritated or driven to anger. A person in whom phlegm was the dominant humor was phlegmatic, or imperturbable. A person in whom blood was dominant was sanguine, or cheerful. A melancholic, or a person with too much black bile, would be prone to depression. We still use the words melancholy, sanguine, choleric, and phlegmatic, though now they refer merely to moods or person-alities and not to the humors once thought to cause these characteristics. All of these humors were thought to be useful. Each contributed something nec-essary to the healthy functioning of the body. If, however, there were too much or too little of any one humor, the imbalance could result in physical or men-tal illness. Furthermore, excess heat in the body, whether it came from an ex-cess of hot humors or from "heated" emotions such as rage, could burn the humors, and these burnt or "adust" humors could be more harmful than the humors in their natural state. Melancholy adust, or burnt melancholy, for ex-ample, could cause not only the depression and grief traditionally associated with melancholy but also fits of rage. The fact that Lear alternates between grief and rage would not have seemed unusual to Shakespeare's contempo-raries if they assumed that he was suffering from melancholy adust. Humoral theory was used to explain many, if not most physical and mental ailments in Shakespeare's day, and melancholy, which could take many forms, appears to have been one of the most commonly diagnosed ailments of the time.

Demon Possession

In the Middle Ages, that is, for several centuries prior to Shakespeare's time, mad people were often said to be possessed by the devil or by evil spirits. Al-though early modern physicians proposed many new explanations of insanity and often argued against the idea of demon-possession as a cause of madness, the theory had not entirely disappeared in Shakespeare's time. In fact, even those physicians who suggested other theories of insanity sometimes incor-porated the idea of demon possession into those theories by suggesting, for example, that certain humors, such as melancholy, make a person more vul-nerable to possession by the devil. Thus, when Edgar disguises himself as "Tom o' Bedlam," a poor, mad beggar released from the insane asylum (1.2.124), he includes in his mad act the mention of many devils and demons, such as "the foul fiend Flibbertigibbet" (3.4.106) and the "foul fiend" that bites his back and "haunts poor Tom in the voice of a nightingale" (3.6.15, 26–7). By frequently mentioning the names of devils and demons who torment him, Edgar made himself into what many of Shakespeare's contemporaries would have imagined a madman to be, a man persecuted and tormented by demons.

Astrology and Cosmology

Astrology and cosmology were also believed to affect mental illness. More than one school of medicine in Shakespeare's day believed that the events of the heavens could affect a person's health, personality, or mental state. Many humoral theorists believed that the planet or heavenly object under which a person was born determined which humor would be dominant in that person. Thus if Saturn was ascendant at a person's birth, that person would be prone to melancholy. Jupiter was thought to control blood, or the sanguine temperament. (Jupiter was another name for the Greek god, Jove; hence a sanguine person is also jovial, a word we still use to mean cheerful.) The sun and Mars were both associated with choler. Likewise the moon and Venus both governed phlegm, and the planet Mercury was thought by some to preside over a "mercurial" or unstable and changeable temperament. Some members of the church opposed astrological theory because it could be interpreted as suggesting that a person's fate was determined by the stars, and not by God. Other theologians, however, asserted that God determined which of the planets would be ascendant at a person's birth, and thus ultimately determined the person's fate. Those philosophers who believed in the free will of humans, as opposed to a fate determined by God or the stars, rejected astrology as superstition. We see references to astrological beliefs in *King Lear* when Gloucester suggests that the recent solar and lunar eclipses are signs of bad luck, and Edmund dismisses this and other beliefs in astrology as superstition:

> This is the excellent foppery of the world, that, when we are sick in fortune, often the surfeit of our own behavior, we make guilty of our disasters the sun, the moon, and the stars; as if we were villains by necessity; fools by heavenly compulsion; knaves, thieves, and treachers, by spherical predominance; drunkards, liars, and adulterers, by an enforced obedience of planetary influence; and all that we are evil in, by a divine thrusting on. An admirable evasion of whoremaster man, to lay his goatish disposition to the charge of a star!...I should have been that I am, had the maidenliest star in the firmament twinkled on my bastardizing. (1.2.109–22)

Edmund here rejects astrological theory, suggesting that it is cowardly to blame one's behavior on a star, or even on the will of God, "a divine thrusting on."

Other schools of medicine rejected humoral theory, but believed in the influence of the heavens on the human mind and body. The Paracelsians, or those physicians who practiced the theories of Paracelsus, an early-sixteenth-century Swiss physician, believed that there was a close relationship and interaction between the microcosm, or small world, of man, and the macrocosm, or large world, of the universe. That is, they believed that people contained the same essential elements that were found in the rest of the universe: sulfur, salt, and mercury; and, therefore, events in the universe could affect people's physical or mental health. The same disturbance of elements that caused an earthquake or thunderstorm might well cause a physical or mental problem in a person. Though Shakespeare more often refers to humoral theory, we do see a few allusions to Paracelsian theory in *King Lear*, most notably in Lear's comparison between the storm outside with its "sulpherous and thought executing fires" and the storm that is raging within him, "the tempest in [his] mind" (3.2.4; 3.4.33).

Stress, Anxiety, and Grief

In the early modern period, as now, tragic events and the stresses and anxieties of everyday life were thought to cause mental disturbances. While some people might weather great losses without any apparent change in mental health, others were driven to depression, melancholy, or extreme anxiety by the loss of a loved one or by the stresses surrounding financial or material loss. The physician William Drage noted in his work *A Physical Nosonomy* (London, 1665) that mental disturbance could be caused by "sadness, fears, and scares, jealousy, discontents betwixt man and wife (the most lacerating of all grief).... loss of love, and disappointment in a marriage, destiny of friends and loss of estates." Many other physicians recited similar lists of emotional stresses that might produce mental disturbances, perhaps by burning the humors or otherwise causing an imbalance in the humoral composition of a person. In the late-sixteenth and early-seventeenth centuries, loved ones, especially children and childbearing women, might easily be carried off by disease or mishap, and economic instability was widespread. Indeed, many of the people who sought the help of a physician, astrologer, or demonologist for mental disorders, either their own or those of others, cited the loss of a loved one, family or marital problems, or economic hardships as the cause of their stress. Thus for Shakespeare's contemporaries, the "unnatural and bemadding sorrow" (3.1.42), which Lear endures in the loss of his kingdom, the betrayal of his family members, and the death of his loved ones would have certainly seemed enough to push Lear to madness.

TREATMENT OF MADNESS

Just as there were many theories about the causes of madness, so there were many treatments of madness in Shakespeare's day. An individual who was mad could be committed to Bethlehem hospital, the name of which came to be pronounced Bethlem and then Bedlam. Bedlam was the first insane asylum in England, and in Shakespeare's time it was the only public hospital dedicated to the care of the insane. Indeed, the word *bedlam* became synonymous with insanity and is still used to describe a chaotic or mad situation. Alternatively, if the mad person had money and property and was declared lunatic by the court of wards (as was nearly the fate of Sir Brian Annesley, mentioned in chapter one) then the court might make the lunatic the ward of a family member or another individual who would then be responsible for caring for the lunatic and managing his or her estate. The quality of such care could vary widely from one guardian to another. Cordell Annesley clearly felt that her sister and brother-in-law would not have been caring guardians for her father, and thus asked that he be given as ward to a family friend if he had to be declared lunatic. Private asylums also existed, and sometimes the mad were kept at home, while others were simply allowed to become vagrants, such as the mad beggar whom Edgar impersonates. When Edgar disguises himself as a "Tom o' Bedlam" he is taking on the role of a mad beggar who has either escaped or been released from Bedlam, clearly without having regained his sanity. Such figures were common in early modern literature and folk songs, and thus would have been familiar to the original audience of Shakespeare's play.

The treatments that the mentally ill might receive at Bedlam or elsewhere were also various. Some patients were whipped or beaten, either in punishment for their behavior or to expel the demons that were thought to be the cause of madness. Patients might also be chained, bound, or imprisoned in a dark room so that they could not escape or behave violently. Other treatments attempted to resolve the humoral imbalance in the mentally ill. Thus a patient might be bled, or vomiting might be induced in order to rid the individual of the excess humor. Diet and herbal remedies might also be used to provide a humor thought to be lacking. Herbal remedies and other medicines were sometimes used to sedate a patient or to help the patient to sleep, as is the case with Lear. And, like Lear's physicians, some doctors believed that music could help to cure madness by soothing the excessive passions that had caused the madness or by inducing whatever passion was missing. Finally, wise counsel or spiritual instruction, such as the advice that Edgar gives to his father to keep him from despair and suicide, might be used in an attempt to steer the patient towards saner behavior.

MELANCHOLY AND MADNESS

Melancholy, or the excess of black bile, was one of the most commonly diagnosed illnesses in Shakespeare's time, and many works were written about it. One of the most widely read and most popular of those works was Robert Burton's *The Anatomy of Melancholy*. In this lengthy work Burton describes the numerous causes, symptoms, and treatments of melancholy, not only stating his own ideas but also citing classical, biblical, and contemporary authorities on the subject. Burton lists a wide variety of possible causes for melancholy, including God's will, evil spirits, immoderate exercise or sleep, the stars, emotions or passions, and age. The first three passages below are excerpts from his discussion of three of these causes: the stars, old age, and sorrow. Burton, however, lists many more causes, and he likewise notes that there were many possible symptoms of melancholy, and that these might vary widely from person to person. The fourth passage below is Burton's description of a few of the symptoms and his explanation of how widely the symptoms might vary from one melancholic to another.

FROM ROBERT BURTON, *THE ANATOMY OF MELANCHOLY,* ED. A. R. SHILLETO, VOL. 1

(London and New York: George Bell and Sons, 1893)

Stars a Cause

Natural causes are either primary and universal, or secondary and more particular. Primary causes are the heavens, planets, stars, etc. by their influence (as our Astrologers hold) producing this and such like effects. I will not stand here to discuss... whether stars be causes, or signs; or to apologize for judicial Astrology.... If thou shalt ask me what I think, I must answer... they do incline, but not compel; no necessity at all... and so gently incline, that a wise man may resist them; ... they rule us, but God rules them. All this (methinks) Joh. De Indagine hath comprised in brief.... "Wilt thou know how far the stars work upon us? I say they do but incline, and that so gently, that if we will be ruled by reason, they have no power over us; but if we follow our own nature, and be led by sense, they do as much in us as in brute beasts, and we are no better." So that, I hope, I may justly conclude with Cajetan... that the heaven is God's instrument, by mediation of which He governs and disposeth these elementary bodies; or a great book, whose letters are the stars, (as one calls it), wherein are written may strange things for such as can read. (235)

Old Age a Cause

The first of these, which is natural to all, and which no man living can avoid, is old age, which being cold and dry, and of the same quality as Melancholy is, must needs cause it, by diminution of spirits and substance, and increasing of adust humours. Therefore Melancthon avers out of Aristotle, as an undoubted truth, *senes plerumque delirasse in senecta,* that old men familiarly dote, *ob atram bilem,* for black choler, which is then superabundant in them: and Rhasis, that Arabian physician...calls it "a necessary and inseparable accident" to all old and decrepit persons. After 70 years (as the Psalmist saith) "all is trouble and sorrow"; and common experience confirms the truth of it in weak and old persons, especially such as have lived in action all their lives, had great employment, much business, much command, and many servants to oversee, and leave off *ex abrupto,* as Charles the Fifth did to King Philip, resign up all of a sudden; they are overcome with melancholy in an instant; or, if they do continue in such courses, they dote at last...and are not able to manage their estates through common infirmities incident in their age; full of ache, sorrow, and grief, children again, dizzards, they carle many times as they sit, and talk to themselves, they are angry, waspish, displeased with everything, "suspicious of all, wayward, covetous, hard" (saith Tully) "self-willed, superstitious, self-conceited, braggers, and admirers of themselves," as Balthasar Castalio hath truly noted of them. (239–40)

Sorrow a Cause of Melancholy

In this Catalogue of Passions, which so much torment the soul of man, and cause this malady (for I will briefly speak of them all, and in their order), the first place in this irascible appetite may justly be challenged by sorrow; an inseparable companion, "the mother and daughter of melancholy her epitome, symptom, and chief cause." As Hippocrates hath it, they beget one another, and tread in a ring, for sorrow is both cause and symptom of this disease. How it is a symptom shall be showed in his place. That it is a cause all the world acknowledgeth.... [sorrow is] a cause of madness, a cause of many other [incurable] diseases, a sole cause of this mischief, Lemnius calls it.... And if it take root once, it ends in despair, as Felix Plater observes...Chrysostom, in his seventeenth epistle to Olympia, describes it to be "a cruel torture of the soul, a most inexplicable grief, poisoned worm, consuming body and soul, and gnawing the very heart, a perpetual executioner, continual night, profound darkness, a whirlwind, a tempest, an ague not appearing, heating worse than any fire, and a battle that hath no end. It crucifies worse than any Tyrant; no torture, no strappado, no bodily punishment, is like unto it".... "It dries up the bones," saith Solomon [*Prov* 17:22] makes them hollow-eyed, pale, and lean, furrow-faced, to have dead looks, wrinkled brows, riveled cheeks, dry bodies, and quite perverts their temperature that are mis-affected with it.... It hinders concoction, refrigerates the heart, takes away stomach, colour, and sleep; thickens the blood...contaminates the spirits...overthrows the natural heat, perverts the good estate of body and mind, and makes them weary of their lives, cry out, howl and roar for the very anguish of their souls. (298–300)

Symptoms of Melancholy

...they will scarce be compelled to do that which concerns them, though it be for their good, so diffident, so dull, of small or no compliment, unsociable, hard to be acquainted with, especially of strangers; they had rather write their minds than speak, and above all things love solitariness.... Are they so solitary for pleasure (one asks) or pain? For both; yet I rather think for fear and sorrow, etc.... they delight in floods and waters, desert places, to walk alone in orchards, gardens, private walks, back-lanes; averse from company...they abhor all companions at last, even their nearest acquaintances and most familiar friends, for they have a conceit (I say) every man observes them, will deride, laugh to scorn, or misuse them, confining themselves therefore wholly to their private houses or chambers.... But this and all precedent symptoms are more or less apparent, as the humour is intended or remitted, hardly perceived in some, or not at all, most manifest in others; childish in some, terrible in others; to be derided in one, pitied or admired in another; to him by fits, to a second continuate; and, howsoever these symptoms be common and incident to all persons, yet they are the more remarkable, frequent, furious, and violent in melancholy men. To speak in a word, there is nothing so vain, absurd, ridiculous, extravagant, impossible, incredible, so monstrous a chimera, so prodigious and strange, such as painters and poets durst not attempt, which they will not really fear, feign, suspect and imagine unto themselves...you may truly say of them in earnest; they will act, conceive in all extremes, contrarieties, and contradictions, and that in infinite varieties.... scarce two of 2000 concur in the same symptoms. The Tower of Babel never yielded such confusion of tongues, as the Chaos of Melancholy doth variety of symptoms. There is in all melancholy...a disagreeing likeness still; and as in a river, we swim in the same place, though not in the same numerical water; as the same instrument affords several lessons, so the same disease yields diversity of symptoms. (454–6)

BEDLAM BEGGARS AND ABRAHAM MEN

Mad Toms, Toms of Bedlam or inmates who had escaped or been released from Bedlam and who now survived by begging, were common characters in sixteenth and seventeenth century folk songs, as were the Abraham men, or imposters who pretended to be mad beggars from Bedlam in order to beg more effectively. The following anonymous folk song is sung from the point of view of a Mad Tom. Since he is mad, much of his song is nonsense. His math, for instance, is illogical. He clearly cannot have been mad for 40 ("twice twenty") of the past 30 years, nor can he have spent 45 of the past 40 years "in durance soundly caged." Nevertheless he does clearly express the experiences of a mad beggar in Shakespeare's day. He sings of his time in the "lovely lofts of Bedlam," where he was "in durance soundly caged," handcuffed in "brave bracelets strong," and subject to "sweet whips" and "wholesome hunger," and he sings of his madness, suggesting by his reference to Cupid, "the roguish boy of love," that love may have been the reason he "fell into this dotage" or madness. He hopes that those he sings to will not, like him, go mad and "be forsaken" of their "five sound senses," and he assures them at the end of the repeated chorus that he is not dangerous, if not crossed, and will "injure nothing." Like Edgar's Mad-Tom character, this lunatic is wild, almost animal-like, and perhaps frightening to those who meet him, though he says he intends no harm, but like Edgar he is also a figure who might evoke pity from many people, as Edgar did from Lear.

ANONYMOUS, "TOM-A-BEDLAM"

(The earliest known version of this song is found in a 1615 manuscript. The version below is from *Wit and Drollery* [London, 1682])

From the hag and hungry goblin,
That into rags would rend ye,
All the spirits that stand
By the naked man,
In the book of moons defend ye.
That of your five sound senses
You never be forsaken,
Nor travel from
Your selves with Tom
Abroad to beg your bacon.
Nor never sing any food and feeding,
Money, drink, or clothing,

Come dame or maid,
Be not afraid,
For Tom will injure nothing.

Of thirty bare years have I
Twice twenty been enraged,
And of forty been
Three times fifteen
In durance soundly caged.
In the lovely lofts of Bedlam,
In stubble soft and dainty,
Brave bracelets strong,
Sweet whips, ding dong,
And a wholesome hunger plenty.
Still I do sing any food and feeding,
Money, drink, or clothing,
Come dame or maid,
Be not afraid,
For Tom will injure nothing.

With a thought I took for Maudlin,
And a cruise of cockle pottage,
And a thing thus—tall
Sky bless you all,
I fell into this dotage;
I slept not till the conquest,
Till then I never waked,
Till the Roguish Boy
Of Love where I lay,
Me found and stript me naked.
And made me sing any food and feeding,
Money, drink, or clothing,
Come dame or maid,
Be not afraid,
For Tom will injure nothing.

When short I have shorn my sow's face,
And swigg'd my horned barrel,
In an oaken inn
Do I pawn my skin,
As a suit of gilt apparel:
The moon's my constant mistress,
And the lovely owl my marrow,
The flaming drake
And the night crow make
Me music to my sorrow.

While there I sing any food and feeding,
Money, drink, or clothing,
Come dame or maid,
Be not afraid,
For Tom will injure nothing.

The palsie plague these pounces,
When I prig your pigs or pullen,
Your culvers take,
Or mateless make
Your Chanticlear and sullen;
When I want provant, with Humphrey I sup;
and when benighted,
To repose in Paul's
With waking souls
I never am affrighted.
For still I do sing any food and feeding,
Money, drink, or clothing,
Come dame or maid,
Be not afraid,
For Tom will injure nothing.

I know more than Apollo,
For oft when he lies sleeping,
I behold the stars
At mortal wars
And the rounded welkin weeping;
The moon embraces her shepherd,
And the Queen of Love her warrior;
While the first does horn
The stars of the morn,
And the next the heavenly farrier.
For still I do sing any food and feeding,
Money, drink, or clothing,
Come dame or maid,
Be not afraid,
For Tom will injure nothing.

The gypsies, Snapp and Pedro,
Are none of Tom's comrades,
The punk I scorn,
And the cut-purse sworn,
And the roaring boys bravado's,
The soler white and gentle
Me trace, or touch and spare not,
But those that cross

Tom's Rhinoceros
Do what the Panther dare not.
Although I sing any food and feeding,
Money, drink, or clothing,
Come dame or maid,
Be not afraid,
For Tom will injure nothing.

With a heart of furious fancies,
Whereof I am commander,
With a burning spear
And a horse of air
To the wilderness I wander,
With a knight of ghosts and shadows
I summoned am to Tourney,
Ten leagues beyond
The wide world's end,
Methinks it is no journey.
All the while I sing any food any feeding,
Money, drink, or clothing,
Come dame or maid,
Be not afraid,
Poor Tom will injure nothing. (149–53)

While some Toms of Bedlam may really have been madmen released or escaped from Bedlam, there were also some beggars who pretended to be "Mad
Toms" in order to beg more money from their frightened or sympathetic con-
tributors. The following description of these Abraham men was written by
Thomas Dekker, a playwright and a writer of prose, roughly contemporary
with Shakespeare. In one of his prose works, *The Belman of London,* he describes various types of rogues, criminals, and con-artists, including the Abraham man. Notice that the Abraham man described repeats "poor Tom is a
cold" just as Edgar does. Edgar, of course, when disguised as Poor Tom, is also
an imposter madman, and Shakespeare may well have borrowed much of his
speech and behavior from that of Abraham men he had seen.

FROM THOMAS DEKKER, *THE BELMAN OF LONDON* (1608),
IN *THE NON-DRAMATIC WORKS OF THOMAS DEKKER,*
VOL. 3, ED. ALEXANDER B. GROSART

(Lancashire: Blackburn, 1885)

Of all the mad rascals (that are of this wing) the *Abraham-man* is the most fantastic: The fellow (quoth this old lady of the *Lake* unto me) that sat half naked (at table

today) from the girdle upward, is the best *Abraham-man* that ever came to my house & the notablest villain: he swears he hath been in Bedlam, and will talk franticly of purpose; you see pins stuck in sundry places of his naked flesh, especially in his arms, which pain he gladly puts himself to (being indeed no torment at all, his skin is either so dead, with some fowl disease, or so hardened with weather,) only to make you believe he is out of his wits. He calls himself by the name of *Poor Tom,* and coming near anybody, cries out, *Poor Tom is a cold.* Of these *Abraham-men,* some be exceeding merry, and do nothing but sing *songs,* fashioned out of their own brains, some will dance, others will do nothing but either laugh or weep, others are dogged and so sullen both in look and speech, that spying but small company in a house, they boldly and bluntly enter, compelling the servants through fear to give them what they demand, which is commonly bacon, or some thing that will yield ready money. The *Upright-man,* and the *Rogue* are not terribler enemies to poultry ware, than *Poor Tom* is; neither does any man shift clean linen oftener than he does his wenches.

PUNISHING MADNESS

Not all of the madmen released or escaped from Bedlam were harmless beggars who would "injure nothing." Even those Toms of Bedlam who were not imposters or Abraham men could be dangerous or disruptive. Some reverted to their mad behavior and caused disturbances in their communities, and therefore the treatment of madness in the early modern period sometimes focused more on punishing the behavior than on curing the disease. In Sir Thomas More's *Apology* he describes a man who was sent to Bedlam (Bedelem) for "beating and correction," and who was then released when his behavior improved. When, however, he began causing disturbances in churches by sneaking up behind praying women and lifting their dresses over their heads, he was bound to a tree and beaten with sticks, or "striped with rods." After this, the author claims, he was better behaved. While such treatment may seem inhumane or ineffective to modern readers, it appears to have been common in Shakespeare's day and explains why Edgar, disguised as Poor Tom, claims to have been "whipped from tithing to tithing, and stocked, punished, and imprisoned" (3.4.141–2). A madman in Shakespeare's time, especially if he were poor and had no one to care for him, might well expect to be whipped, imprisoned, or otherwise punished for his madness.

FROM SIR THOMAS MORE, *THE APOLOGYE OF SYR T. MORE KNYGHT*, CHAPTER 36 (1533)

(London, 1533, 197–99)

Another was one, which after that he had fallen into the frantic heresies, fell soon after into plain open frenzy beside. And all be it that he had therefore been put up in Bedelem, and afterward by beating and correction gathered his remembrance to him, and began to come again to himself, being thereupon set at liberty and walking about abroad, his old fancies began to fall again in his head. And I was from diverse good holy places advertised, that he used in his wandering about, to come into the church, & there make many mad toys & trifles, to the trouble of good people in the divine service, and specially would he be most busy in the time of most silence, while the priest was at the secretes of the mass. . . . And if he spied any woman kneeling at a form, if her head hung any thing low in her meditations, then would he steal behind her, & if he were not letted [stopped] would labor to lift up all her clothes & cast them quite over her head. Whereupon I being advertised of the pageants, and being sent unto and required by very devout religious folk, to take some other order with him / caused him as he came wandering by my door, to be taken by the constables and bound to a tree in the street before the whole town, and there they striped him with rods therefore till he waxed weary and somewhat longer. And it appeared well that his remembrance was good enough, save that it went about in grazing till it was beaten home. For he could then very well rehearse his faults himself and speak and treat very well, and promise to do afterward as well. And verily god be thanked I hear none harm of him now.

COUNSEL AND DIET

Not all treatment of madness involved punishment or imprisonment. In Sir Thomas Elyot's *The Castle of Health* he discusses some of the causes and treatments of various forms of mental illness, and he recommends a combination of counseling to help sooth the strong emotions that might cause mental imbalance and herbal remedies and healthful diet to help restore the natural humoral balance.

Elyot notes that extreme passions, or emotions, can cause mental illness, and he also makes reference to humoral theory when he claims that sorrow "exhausts both natural heat and moisture of the body." He thus recommends herbal remedies that will "expel melancholic humors" or help to purge the black bile from the body, and he suggests a diet that will produce "blood clear and fine," not containing an excess of black bile.

Some of his advice may not seem helpful to us, and it is doubtful whether even in Shakespeare's time grieving parents would have been consoled for the death of their children by the reminder that many living children turn out bad and cause their parents much grief, but Elyot is at least suggesting a compassionate remedy for madness rather than a mere punishment of mad behavior.

FROM SIR THOMAS ELYOT, *THE CASTLE OF HEALTH* (1541)

(London, 1541)

Of Affects of the Mind, Book 3, Chapter 11

...not the least part to be considered...is of affects and passions of the mind. For if they be immoderate, they do not only annoy the body, & shorten the life, but also.... they bring a man from the use of reason, and sometime in the displeasure of almighty god. Wherefore they do not only require the help of physic corporal, but also the counsel of a man wise and well learned in moral philosophy. Wherefore after that I have recited, what they be, I will briefly declare such counsels, as I have gathered. And as concerning remedies of physic saving a few simples, which do comfort the heart & spirits, the residue I will remit to the counsel of physicians.... Affects of the mind, whereby the body is annoyed, and do bring in sickness, be these, ire or wrath, heaviness or sorrow, gladness, or rejoicing. (62)

Of Dolor or Heaviness of Mind, Book 3, Chapter 12

There is nothing more enemy to life, than sorrow, called also heaviness, for it exhausts both natural heat and moisture of the body, and does extenuate or make the body lean, dulls the wit, and darkens the spirits, letteth [restricts] the use and judgment of reason, and oppresses memory. And Salomon says that sorrow dries up the bones. And also, like as the moth in the garment, and the worm in the tree, so does heaviness annoy the heart of a man.... sorrow hath killed many, and in itself is found no commodity.

Also by heaviness death is hastened, it hides virtue or strength, and heaviness of heart bows down the neck. This is so puissant an enemy to nature and bodily health, that to resist the malice and violence thereof, are required remedies, as well of the wholesome counsels found in holy scripture, and in the books of moral doctrine, as also of certain herbs, fruits, and spices, having the property to expel melancholic humors, and to comfort and keep lively the spirits, which have their proper habitation in the heart of man and moderate nourishing of the natural heat and humor called radical, which is the base of foundation, whereupon the life of man stands, and that failing, life falls in ruin, & the body is dissolved. Now first I will declare some remedies against sorrowfulness of heart, concerning necessary counsel....

If death of children be cause of thy heaviness, call to thy remembrance some children (of whom there is no little number) whose lives either for incorrigible vices, or unfortunate chances, have been more grievous unto their parents, than the death of thy children, ought to be unto thee: considering that death is the discharger of all griefs and miseries, and to them that die well, the first entry in to life everlasting.

The loss of goods or authority do grieve none but fools, which do not mark diligently, that like as neither the one nor the other doth always happen to them that are worthy, so we have in daily experience, that they fall from him suddenly, who in increasing, or keeping them seems most busy.

Oftentimes the repulse from promotion is cause of discomfort, but then consider, whether in the opinion of good men, thou art deemed worthy to have such advancement, or in thyne own expectation and fantasy. If good men so judge thee, thank thou god of that felicity, and laugh at the blindness of them, that so have refused thee. If it proceed of thyne own folly, abhor all arrogance, and enforce thy self to be advanced in men's estimation, before thou canst find thy self worthy in thy proper opinion.

This now shall suffice concerning remedies of moral philosophy. Now will I write somewhat touching the counsel of physic, as in relieving the body, which either by the said occasions, or by the humor of melancholy is brought out of temper.

The first counsel is, that during the time of that passion, eschew to be angry, studious, or solitary, and rejoice thee with melody, or else be always in such company, as best may content thee.

Avoid all things that be noxious in sight, smelling, and hearing, and embrace all thing that is delectable.

Flee darkness, much watch, and busyness of mind, much companying with women, the use of things very hot and dry...immoderate exercise, thirst, much abstinence, dry winds and cold.

Abstain from daily eating of much old beef or old mutton, hard cheese, hare flesh . . . venison, salt fish . . . very coarse bread, great fishes of the sea . . . wine red and thick, meats being very salty . . . garlic, onions, or leeks.

Use meats, which are temperately hot, and therewith somewhat moist, boiled rather than roasted, light of digestion, and engendering blood clear and fine. . . . (64–8)

MUSIC AND MADNESS

In act four, scene seven of *King Lear,* Cordelia implores the gods to heal her father:

O, you kind gods,
Cure this great breach in his abused nature!
Th' untuned and jarring senses, O, wind up,
Of this child-changed father.

Her reference to his untuned and jarring senses suggests that his mind is like a musical instrument in need of tuning, and a few lines later the physicians will attempt to cure Lear with the use of music. This echoes the ideas of the Italian philosopher and physician, Marsilio Ficino, who suggested that music could be used to cure madness, the harmony of the music restoring the inner harmony of the mind. These ideas were also voiced by English writers such as John Case, a musician and physician. In the following excerpt from his *The Praise of Musicke,* Case argues that music can be used to cure both mental and physical ills and to drive out evil spirits, and he cites several examples from classical literature and the Bible as well as from the common experience of using music to relieve sorrow.

FROM JOHN CASE, *THE PRAISE OF MUSICKE* (1586)

(Oxenford, 1586)

The effects of music generally are these. To make haste to incite and stir up men's courage, to allay & pacify anger, to move pity and compassion, and to make pleasant and delightsome. Nay yet I will go farther. I doubt not but to prove by good authority, that music hath brought mad men into their perfect wits and senses, that it hath cured diseases, driven away evil spirits, yea and also abandoned the pestilence from men and cities. (56–7)

...we daily prove it in our selves, using Music as a medicine for our sorrow, and a remedy for our grief. For as every disease is cured by his contrary, so music is as an Antipharmacon to sorrow, abandoning pensive and heavy cogitations, as the sun beams do the lightsome vapors. Greater are those other properties of this art, which I will in this place rather touch than dilate with examples. Music assuages and eases the inordinate perturbations and evil affections of the mind. For Pythagoras with the changing of the sound of his instrument, caused a young man overcome with the impatience of love to change his affection also, wholly taking away the extremity of his passion. So Empedocles with his skilful playing on the Cittern hindered a mad man, ready to slay himself. Yea Zencrates also and Alclepiades, are said by this only medicine to have restored a lunatic person, into his perfect senses. If it be so that music can help the outrages of the mind, it will not seem incredible that it should cure the diseases of the body. By the help of music Ismenias a Theban musician, restored men sick of an ague, to their former health, and Asclepiades by the sound of a trumpet caused a deaf man to hear....

It is also a present remedy against evil Spirits, which as it is proved by that one example of Saul from whom the evil Spirit departed when David played on his Harp, so having so sufficient authority for the confirmation thereof, I shall not need to stand upon it any longer. (61–2)

VISITS TO BEDLAM

St. Mary of Bethlehem hospital, more commonly known by its corrupted name, Bedlam, was established in 1247 and became the first hospital devoted exclusively to the care and housing of the insane. But while the inmates were provided with food and shelter, curing their madness was not always the only activity or even the first priority of the hospital. During the early modern period, visits to Bedlam to see the mad people were a popular form of entertainment. The following two documents illustrate some of the problems with this form of amusement, which turned the sufferings of the mad into a spectacle for bored visitors. Thomas Dekker along with Thomas Middleton wrote a play titled *The Honest Whore,* in which a duke and some of his courtiers visit Bedlam and view the inmates. The first madman they encounter is obsessively mourning the loss of his ships at sea many years ago, and while the visitors express some pity for him, they also find his raving amusing. Like Gloucester in *King Lear,* the madman reminds them that they should pity and respect him because he is so old and has a "grey beard and head," but they continue to "mock old age" and the madman is threatened with whipping if he does not behave.

FROM THOMAS DEKKER AND THOMAS MIDDLETON, *THE HONEST WHORE,* PART 1

(London, 1605)

Scene 15

Castruchio: Pray may we see some of those wretched souls
That here are in your keeping?
Anselmo: Yes, you shall,
But, gentlemen, I must disarm you then,
There are of madmen, as there are of tame,
All humoured not alike. We have here some,
So apish and fantastic, play with a feather,
And though 'twould grieve a soul to see God's image,
So blemished and defaced, yet do they act
such antic and such pretty lunacies,
That spite of sorrow, they will make you smile.
Others again we have like hungry Lions,
Fierce as wild bulls, untameable as flies,
And these have oftentimes from strangers' sides

Snatched rapiers suddenly, and done much harm,
Whom if you'll see, you must be weaponless.

All: With all our hearts.

Anselmo:....
Stand off a little, pray—so, so, 'tis well.
I'll show you here a man that was sometimes,
A very grave and wealthy citizen,
Has served an apprenticeship to this misfortune:
Been here seven years, and dwelled in Bergamo.

Duke: How fell he from his wits?

Anselmo: By loss at sea.
I'll stand aside, question him you alone,
For if he spy me, he'll not speak a word
Unless he's throughly vex'd
[He reveals an old man wrapped in a net]

Fluello: Alas, poor soul.

Castruchio: A very old man.

Duke: God speed, father.

1st Madman: God speed the plough: thou shalt not speed me!

Pioratto: We see you, old man, for all you dance in a net.

1st Madman: True, but thou wilt dance in a halter, and I shall not see thee.

Anselmo: Oh, do not vex him, pray

Castruchio: Are you a fisherman, father?

1st Madman: No, I'm neither fish nor flesh.

Fluello: What do you with that net then?

1st Madman: Dost not see, fool? There's a fresh salmon in't. If you step one foot further, you'll be over shoes, for you see I'm over head and ear in the salt-water. And if you fall into this whirlpool where I am, you are drowned, you are a drowned rat. I am fishing here for five ships, but I cannot have a good draught, for my net breaks still, and breaks, but I'll break some of your necks and I catch you in my clutches. Stay, stay, stay, stay, stay—where's the wind, where's the wind, where's the wind, where's the wind? Out, you gulls, you goose caps, you gudgeon eaters! Do you look for wind in the heavens? Ha, ha, ha, ha! No, No! Look there, look there, look there, the wind is always at that door. Hark how it blows , poof, poof, poof.

All: Ha, ha, ha.

1st Madman: Do you laugh at God's creatures? Do you mock old age, you rogues? Is this gray beard and head counterfeit, that you cry "Ha, ha, ha"?—Sirrah, art not thou my eldest son?

Pioratto: Yes indeed father.

1st Madman: Then thou art a fool, for my eldest son had a pole foot, crooked legs, a verges face, and a pear coloured beard. I made him a scholar, and he made himself a fool. Sirrah, thou there? Hold out thy hand.

Duke: My hand? Well, here 'tis.

1st Madman: Look, look, look, look. Has he not long nails and short hair?

Fluello: Yest monstrous short hair, and abominable long nails.

1st Madman: Ten penny nails are they not?

Fluello: Yes, ten penny nails.

1st Madman: Such nails had my second boy. Kneel down thou varlet, and ask thy father's blessing. Such nails had my middlemost son and I made him a promoter. And he scraped, and scraped, and scraped, till he got the devil and all. But he scraped thus and thus, and thus, and it went under his legs, till at length a company of Kites taking him for carrion, swept up all, all, all, all, all, all, all. If you love your loves, look to your selves. See, see, see, see. The Turks' galleys are fighting with my ships. "Bounce" goes the guns, "oooh" cry the men, "rumble, rumble" go the waters.—Alas, there! 'Tis sunk, 'Tis sunk. I am undone. I am undone, you are the damned pirates have undone me. You are, by th' Lord, you are, you are, stop 'em, you are!

Anselmo: Why, how now, sirrah! Must I fall to tame you?

1st Madman: Tame me! No, I'll be madder than a roasted cat. See, see, I am burnt with gunpowder. These are our close fights.

Anselmo: I'll whip you, if you grow unruly thus.

1st Madman: Whip me? Out you toad! Whip me? What justice is this, to whip me because I'm a beggar? Alas! I am a poor man, a very poor man! I am starved, and have had no meat by this light, ever since the great flood, I am a poor man.

Anselmo: Well, well, be quiet, and you shall have meat.

1st Madman: Ay, I pray do; for look you, here be my guts; these are my ribs—you may look through my ribs—see how my guts come out? These are my red guts, my very guts, oh, oh!

Anselmo: Take him in there

All: A very piteous sight

Castruchio: Father, I see you have a busy charge.

Anselmo: They must be used like children,
pleased with toys,
and anon whipped for their unruliness.

Modern readers of plays such as *King Lear* or *The Honest Whore,* may understand the early modern fascination with madness. We, after all, are also viewing a spectacle of madness by reading these plays. Nevertheless, many may find the visiting of Bedlam to laugh at the inmates a cruel form of entertainment. Such sentiments may have been shared by some of Shakespeare's contemporaries, as well. Even *The Honest Whore* can be interpreted as a subtle criticism of the practice, since the madman rebukes his visitors for laughing at his misfortune. But only 70 years later, in 1689, did Thomas Tryon author the first published condemnation of visits to Bedlam. Tryon argues that the practice, which continued to be popular, was counterproductive and prevented the cure of madness while also exposing the inmates to teasing and ridicule.

FROM THOMAS TRYON, *A TREATISE OF DREAMS AND VISIONS, TO WHICH IS ADDED A DISCOURSE OF THE CAUSES, NATURES AND CURE OF PHRENSIE, MADNESS OR DISTRACTION*

(London, 1689)

And as stupefying medicines are of little value, but rather prejudicial, so, much more mischievous is too much company, and prating, and especially, the teasing of such distempered people with unnecessary questions; on which score, as I must acknowledge that gallant structure of *New Bethlam* to be one of the prime ornaments of the city of *London,* and a noble monument of *Charity,* so I would with all humility beg the honorable and worthy governors thereof, that they would be pleased to use some effectual means, for restraining their inferior officers, from admitting such swarms of people, of all ages and degrees, for only a little paltry profit to come in there, and with their noise, and vain questions to disturb the poor souls; as especially such, as do resort thither on holy-days, and such spare time, when for several hours (almost all day long) they can never be at any quiet, for those importunate visitants, whence manifold great inconveniences do arise. For, first, 'tis a very indecent, inhumane thing to make, as it were, a show of those unhappy objects of charity committed to their care, (by exposing them, and naked too perhaps of either sex) to the idle curiosity of every vain boy, petulant wench, or drunken companion, going along from one apartment to the other, and crying out; this woman is in for love; that man for jealousy. He has over-studied himself, and the like. Secondly, this staring rabble seldom fail of asking more than an hundred impertinent questions.—As, what are you here for? How long have you been here, &c. which most times enrages the distracted person, though calm and quiet before, and then the poor creature falls a raving and too probably a cursing and swearing, and so the holy and tremendous name of God is dishonored, whilst the wicked people, who think it a diversion, instead of trembling, as indeed they ought, being themselves really guilty of all these blasphemies, fall a laughing and hooting, and so the poor distracted creatures become twice more fierce and violent than ever.

Thirdly, as long as such disturbances are suffered, there is little hope that any cure of medicine should do them good to reduce them to their senses or right minds, as we call it, and so the very principle end of the house is defeated. Certainly the most hopeful means towards their recovery would be to keep them with a clean spare diet, and as quiet as may be, and to let none come at them but their particular friends, grave sober people and such as they have a kindness for, and those too, not always, but only at proper times whereby discoursing with them in their lucid intervals gravely, soberly, and discreetly, and humoring them in little things, shall do much more I am confident, toward their cure, then most of the medicines that are commonly administered. (289–93)

LUNACY AND THE COURT OF WARDS

A madman who had property might be declared lunatic and deprived of that property by the court of wards. The court would investigate the charges of lunacy, determine whether the person was capable of managing his estate, and if it were determined that he was not able, appoint a guardian to care for him and to reap the benefits of his estate. This was the fate that might have awaited Sir Brian Annesley (see chapter one) had his daughter, Cordell, not intervened on his behalf, and a similar fate befell Lear since he gave his estate to his daughters and was then forced to depend on them to care for him. The following document demonstrates the process that was followed in order to determine whether a person was capable of caring for himself and managing his estate.

FROM THE CASE OF EDMUND FRANCKLIN A LUNATIC (C. 1630), BEDFORD COUNTRY RECORD OFFICE, FRANCKLIN MS, FN 1060–84. SEE *THREE HUNDRED YEARS OF PSYCHIATRY: 1535–1860: A HISTORY PRESENTED IN SELECTED ENGLISH TEXTS,* ED. RICHARD HUNTER AND IDA MACALPINE

(London, New York: Oxford University Press, 1963)

Edmund Francklin of Bolnhurst in the Country of Bedford Esqr. By Inquisition bearing date the 9th of January 3 Caroli. Committed to George Francklin, Nicholas Francklin and John Francklin his Brothers.

The said Edmund Francklin hath ever since the said commitment been violent & outrageous in his carriage divers several times sometimes more sometimes less, and within the space of two years last past hath divers several times behaved himself in manner following.

Disturbed the minister in the church when he was preaching several times within the space aforesaid. And in the church in divine service in July last, at sermon time, used these words, that his brother George was God the Father, his son, God the Sonne and the Lady Dyer God the Holy Ghost. He hath divers times...said that he was God, that he suffered more than Christ, that the wine at this own table was better than the communion, not suffer grace to be said at his table, nor prayers in his house as was customably and duly used heretofore. He hath...spoke unfittingly of diverse Noblemen and Gentlemen in the Country, and of his father and mother, and saying that he killed his father and two of his sisters and would kill the rest meaning his brothers before he had done. He hath...often broke glass windows and divers bays of walls, threw divers things of value secretly into the fire; and some into the ponds, and as he sat at meat would mangle and cut the meat unfittingly and throw it to the dogs. About a month before Christmas last he fell upon Mr. Roper, a gentleman whom Mr. Fitzgeoffry brought to his house, threw him down and stabbed at him with a knife because he seemed to contradict him when he said he was his God...Since Easter last he hath fallen with violence upon his brother...threw a great iron jack winch, and a great stone at him, threatened to shoot him, to cut his throat and to kill him...he continually lay in wait for him...

During the time of this his commitment he never meddled with his estate received no rents, nor disposed of his lands either by letting or other managing...and by the opinion of all the country that are understanding and have heard of or seen his Carriage, thought unfit to manage his estate. The said Edmund Francklin so demeaning himself and being in such estate and there being divers plots upon him to marry him unworthily, and to draw him into greater expenses than his estate would bear, for preventing of these mischiefs and restraining his dangerous violence the said George Francklin one of the committees in the present of Mr. Richard Taylor and Nicholas Franklin another of the committees made complaint about the latter end of Trinity term last to the attorney of the Court of Wards, of the danger his person was in, in respect of the said plots, and his estate by such expenses, and of his carriage & demeanor in general, and of his particular carriage to him, and made affidavit thereof and thereupon had an order for his restraint.

The said George Francklin by the advice and consent of Mr. Richard Taylor, and of Nicolas Francklin another of the committee did agree with Dr. Crooke, Censor of the College of Physicians, Sworn Servant to King James, and entrusted by the King with the government of the great Hospital of Bethlehem in London for to pay him after the rate of two hundred pounds a year for the physic, diet, clothes, lodging, washing and all things necessary for the said Edmund, and two men servantes to attend upon him, so long as the said Edmund Francklin should be with him. And thereupon the said Doctor Crooke came down...from London in his coach and four horses, attended with three men and came to the house, and did see what & in what manner it was done, and finding him in bed entreated him fairly, caused him to make him ready, and to break his fast and carried him to London to the doctor's own house where he was fairly entreated and well used & carefully provided of a good lodging and wholesome and good diet, according to the quality of his person and nature of his infirmity. (103–5)

QUESTIONS FOR WRITTEN AND ORAL DISCUSSION

1. Look up the words "melancholy," "sanguine," "jovial," "phlegmatic," and "choleric." Which of the characters in this play do these words seem to describe?

2. Examine the symptoms of Melancholy that Burton lists. Which characters in the play possess these qualities? Does the character possess all of the symptoms listed?

3. Burton notes that sorrow is both a cause and a symptom of melancholy. Which of Lear's and/or Gloucester's sorrows do you think may have caused their madness and which are a result of their madness?

4. Burton lists many possible causes of melancholy. Excerpts of his discussion of three of these causes have been provided for you. Which of these causes (sorrow, the stars, and old age) do you think causes melancholy, or madness, in *King Lear?*

5. Compare Burton's discussion of the effects of the stars on melancholy with Edmund's statements about astrology (act one, scene two). How do they differ? In what ways are they similar? What would Edgar have thought of Burton's statements?

6. Burton suggests that old age can be a cause of melancholy. To what extent is old age the cause of the madness of Lear and Gloucester? What similarities do you find between these characters and the symptoms Burton describes?

7. In act one, scene one, Regan suggests that Lear is becoming senile, but she also says that he has "ever but slenderly known himself" (1.1.291). Kent and Gloucester, however, claim that Lear's "wits begin to unsettle" only because of the actions of Regan and Goneril (3.4.149). When does Lear go mad? Is he mad at the beginning of the play or does his madness occur later? Support your opinion with evidence from the text.

8. Compare the Mad Tom of the folk song and the Abraham man that Dekker describes with Edgar's Poor Tom. How are they similar? How are they different? Do you think Edgar is pretending to be a real madman, or is he pretending to be an imposter? Why do you think Edgar chose this disguise?

9. Examine Sir Thomas More's description of the madman who was whipped for his disruptive behavior. Do you think he should have been whipped? How would you treat such behavior?

10. What do you think of Sir Thomas Elyot's advice? How could it be improved? What advice would you give to people in the situations he describes? What advice would you give to the characters in *King Lear?*

11. Which characters in *King Lear* attempt to give counsel or advice to people in danger of madness? What do you think of their advice? How does it compare with the advice offered by Elyot?

12. Look at act four, scene seven, in light of John Case's *Praise of Musick.* How would you stage this scene if you wanted to show that music helped to cure Lear's madness?

13. John Case argues that music can cure madness and disease, and music therapy is still practiced today. Can you think of times when music has comforted you, calmed you, or cheered you up? Do different types of music have different effects on your moods?

14. Stage your own spectacle of madness with classmates playing the parts of mad characters from *King Lear.* Which characters would be found in your version of Bedlam? How would they behave? Why might people be interested in seeing such a spectacle?

15. Tryon condemns the practice of allowing visitors to view the inmates of Bedlam for entertainment. What do you think of the practice? Would you want to visit such a place? Why or why not? What similarities does watching a play about madness have to such a visit? How is it different?

16. Look up the word "bedlam" in a dictionary. What does it currently mean? What scenes from *King Lear* could best be described by the word "bedlam"?

17. Look at the letters from Brian Annesley's case (chapter one) and the letter regarding the case of Edmund Francklin. With these letters in mind, choose one character from the play and argue whether or not you feel that character should be declared a lunatic and deprived of his or her estate. One team of students should argue for the lunacy of the character while another group argues for the competency of that character.

SUGGESTED READING

Hoeniger, David F. *Medicine and Shakespeare in the English Renaissance.* Newark, NJ: U of Delaware P, 1992.

Hunter, Richard, and Ida Macalpine. *Three Hundred Years of Psychiatry 1535–1860.* Hartsdale, NY: Carlisle, 1982.

Kail, Aubrey C. *The Medical Mind of Shakespeare.* Balgowlah, NSW, Australia: Williams and Wilkins, 1986.

Lindsay, Jack. ed. *Loving Mad Tom: Bedlamite Verse of the XVI and XVII Centuries.* London: Fanfrolico Press, 1927.

Reed, Robert. *Bedlam on the Jacobean Stage.,* Cambridge: Harvard UP, 1952.

Tuke, Daniel Hack. *Chapters in the History of the Insane in the British Isles.* London: Kegan, Paul, Trench & Co, 1882.

3

Kingship: The Responsibilities and Weaknesses of a Ruler

King Lear is, as its title suggests, a play about a king, but it is not simply a play about the historical and legendary King Lear. In many ways it is also about King James, the King of England and Scotland at the time that Shakespeare wrote *King Lear.*

King Lear is a very politically sensitive play. In it we see hints of a lot of the hot political issues of the day, especially issues concerning the new king, James I, who was a rather controversial figure in his day. In the play Shakespeare alludes to some of the controversies surrounding James, and he gives Lear some of James's own weaknesses; however, he also promotes some of James's pet projects and endows Lear with some of the characteristics that James thought he and all kings should have. He also gives Lear a fool, and James I was the first English king since Henry VIII to have an official court fool; Shakespeare even gives Lear's two sons-in-law the titles of James's two sons. James's eldest son, Henry, was the Duke of Cornwall, and his younger son, Charles, was the Duke of Albany. This chapter will introduce students to King James, the controversies that surrounded him, and the goals he tried to achieve, and it will also illuminate the similarities and differences between Lear and James. Finally, documents written by or about James will be provided so that students can see how James was viewed in his own time, and how a play that alluded to him and his concerns might have been viewed and understood. In most cases spelling and punctuation have been modernized for the sake of clarity.

THE CONTROVERSIAL NEW KING

Queen Elizabeth I ruled England for most of Shakespeare's life. She ruled 1558–1603, but she never married and left no children to inherit her throne.

This meant that in her latter years the English were in doubt about who would rule after her. She had often been encouraged to marry, but she had refused, nor would she agree to name an heir. It was rumored, however, that on her deathbed she named her cousin, James, as her successor, and indeed he had been considered the heir apparent for some time, as he was the Queen's cousin. He was, however, already King James VI of Scotland, and had been king there since he was five years old. Thus his succession to the English throne made him King James VI of Scotland and King James I of England simultaneously.

His English subjects appear to have been relieved at the peaceful transition to a new monarch after so many years of concern about the vulnerability of the nation should Elizabeth die and leave the country without a king; nevertheless, they also had their concerns about the new king.

As a Scot, James was a foreigner in England, and in the early seventeenth century the differences between England and Scotland were immense. Although they occupied the same island, they were two separate nations. (Imagine how citizens of the two countries would feel if the prime minister of Canada were also elected president of the United States.) The English were not entirely certain they trusted a Scot as king, and they feared that he would favor his Scottish subjects. To some extent, this does seem to have been a problem. James made many of his fellow Scots knights, and appointed others to important positions. This was troubling not only because it showed favoritism, but also because knighthood was supposed to be earned, usually by military prowess and valor, and James was merely making knights of his friends and countrymen without regard to merit. In this respect he was similar to Lear, who is not always a good judge of character, and who rewards those who flatter him rather than those who are most loyal to him. James's favoring of the Scots did diminish over time, but he always had certain "favorites," men who were close to him, received favors from him, and often, had sexual affairs with him. James was married and had children, but he was mainly attracted to men. This again caused controversy not only because of the sexual scandal at the time but also because of fears that James would allow his favorites to influence his policies or that he would be too generous with his gifts to them and would so deplete the nation's treasury.

The depletion of the nation's treasury, in fact, was another of the concerns about James. He had no gift for finances, as even he admitted, and he tended to be very generous with money as long as he hadn't actually seen the money. Money that was in his own possession was much harder to obtain. Upon first becoming King of England, James did, of course, have necessary expenses. A new king is expected to celebrate, and to treat his subjects and foreign ambassadors to a celebration, and James did so. Even after his coronation, however, his expenditures remained high. He was fond of holding court masques, a form of entertainment in which nobles would act and dance for the audience, and he spent a great deal of money on the costumes and settings for these masques. Again, in this respect James resembled Lear, who enjoys the pleasures of being king, but is not always willing to accept the responsibilities of caring for his subjects. Indeed, Lear realizes when he is on the heath that he has "taken too little care" of the poor in his kingdom, and that he should "shake the superflux" or give some of his excessive wealth, to them (3.4.33–6).

Like Lear, James was not always adept at dealing with his subjects, and he also had difficulty working with Parliament. He hated crowds, and unlike Queen Elizabeth, he did not like making public appearances, which disappointed the English people who liked seeing the king. He also had some difficulties in dealing with Parliament, which made it more difficult for him to accomplish his goals as king.

But with all these controversies and weaknesses, James also had his strengths as a king. He was very fond of theater and was a great patron of the arts. Indeed, Shakespeare's acting troupe, until then known as The Chamberlain's Men, was renamed The King's Men, and Shakespeare in effect became the court dramatist. Many of Shakespeare's earlier plays were revived and performed for James and the royal family, and his new plays were also sometimes performed at court. In fact, the first recorded performance of *King Lear* was, according to the title page of an early edition of the play, "before the Kings Majestie at Whitehall upon S. Stephans night in Christmas Holidays." James was, furthermore, extremely well educated and intelligent, and exceptionally intellectual for a king. He wrote several books and treatises, which, together with his speeches, leave us a clear record of his hopes, ideas, goals, and intentions, and among his primary goals were peace whenever possible and the union of Scotland and England as one nation.

The latter, of course, is also alluded to in *King Lear.* In his first parliament, James declared his desire to unite the kingdoms of Scotland and England as one realm, Great Britain, restoring the ancient title and unity. He failed to get parliamentary support, but continued to argue for the union for many years. *King Lear* was written only a year or two after James's coronation and first parliament, and so when Lear says, "Know, that we have divided / In three our kingdom" (1.1.33–4) it would have resonated with Shakespeare's audience, reminding them that the kingdom used to be unified, and that it shouldn't have been divided to begin with.

As a member of The King's Men, of course, Shakespeare would have had reason to want to please his patron, and in addition to alluding to one of James's pet projects, Shakespeare creates a king who, for all his flaws, also embodies much of what James thought a king should be. James was a fervent believer in the divine right of kings. That is, he believed that kings were God's representatives on earth, were given by God the right to rule, and were above the law, being, as they were, the creators of the law. While Lear makes many mistakes as king, he does seem to possess an innate "authority" (1.4.27). There is something about him that makes his followers desire to serve him, or as Kent, disguised as Caius tells him, "you have that in your countenance that I would fain call master" (1.4.24–5). Indeed, the very willful way in which he makes his mistakes, deciding to divide his kingdom without even consulting with his advisors, for example, suggests that he is a king by divine right. He is above the law and can make decisions that affect the welfare of the Kingdom without even consulting his counselors. While James I might have criticized some of Lear's foolish decisions, he would have acknowledged the right of a king to make those decisions and to enforce them.

KING JAMES ON KINGSHIP

The following three documents are from books written by or speeches given by King James I, and all three illustrate his own views of kingship and the divine right of kings. The first two, *The True Law of Free Monarchies* and *Basilicon Doron* were both written while James was King of Scotland but before he had become King of England. In *The True Law of Free Monarchies* James draws upon biblical references to kings to show that kings are chosen and placed upon the throne by God, and that they therefore have certain God-given rights and responsibilities. He also compares kings to fathers, noting that it is the duty of kings to care for their subjects and to discipline them as a loving father would.

Basilicon Doron, the title of which comes from a Greek phrase meaning "kingly gift," was written by James for his eldest son, Henry. Being the eldest son, Henry was expected to inherit the crown after James, but he died young. In this book James instructs his son on the responsibilities and duties of kings, and he again asserts his belief in the divine right of kings. In the opening poem, James says that God gives kings the "style of Gods," that is, kings are like gods in relation to their subjects because God has placed kings in a position of power. Note, however, in the second excerpt from this book, that James also differentiates between good and bad kings, or between good kings and tyrants. A good king, he argues, will put the well-being of his subjects and his country before his own happiness or ambitions. Because of this his subjects will mourn his death and he will be long remembered as a good king, while the death of a tyrant king who is more interested in his own ambitions than in his people's happiness will be a relief to his subjects. Though kings are given their power and privileges by God, they are also given certain responsibilities, which they must fulfill.

The last of these three documents is a speech that James delivered to Parliament on March 21, 1609. In this speech, given six years after James became King of England, it is clear that he still believes in the divine right of kings. Indeed, his emphasis on that doctrine is even stronger in this speech than in his earlier treatises. Once again James compares kings to gods and to fathers, and he also compares the king of a realm to the head of a body, but in this speech he emphasizes the power of kings over their subjects. The father with whom he compares the king is not described as a gentle, generous father who thinks first of the welfare of his children, but as a father who has the ability to disinherit them if he wishes. Likewise in comparing kings to gods James here emphasizes the power of God to give and take life, to judge and to be beyond judgment. Toward the end of the following excerpt James does modify his statements by noting that God would not destroy his creation and a father would not disinherit his children without cause, but overall the speech enforces James's views on the power and rights of kings rather than enumerating their responsibilities and duties. In all three of these documents, James describes his views on what a king should be, and in all three we can see some of the characteristics of King Lear. It should be noted, however, that King Lear also bears some resemblance to the tyrant-king and to the father who disinherits his children without cause. Lear embodies many of the characteristics that James admired and thought a king should embody, but he also exhibits some of the negative qualities that James would have criticized.

FROM *THE TRUE LAW OF FREE MONARCHIES: OR THE RECIPROCAL AND MUTUAL DUTY BETWIXT A FREE KING, AND HIS NATURAL SUBJECTS* (1598), IN *THE POLITICAL WORKS OF JAMES I*, ED. CHARLES HOWARD MCILWAIN

(Cambridge: Harvard University Press, 1918)

First then, I will set down the true grounds, whereupon I am to build, out of the Scriptures, since *Monarchy* is the true pattern of Divinity, as I have already said: Next, from the fundamental Laws of our own Kingdome, which nearest must concern us: thirdly, from the law of Nature, by divers similitudes drawn out of the same....

The Prince's duty to his Subjects is clearly set down in many places of the Scriptures, and so openly confessed by all the good Princes, according to their oath in their Coronation, as not needing to be long therein, shall as shortly as I can run through it....

Kings are called Gods by the prophetical King *David*, because they sit upon God his Throne in the earth, and have the count of their administration to give unto him [Psalms 82.6]. Their office is, *To minister Justice and Judgment to the people,* [Psalms 101] as the same *David* saith: To advance the good, and punish the evil, [Psalms 101] as he likewise saith: *To establish good Laws to his people, and procure obedience to the same,* [2 Kings 18] as divers good Kings of *Judah* did [2 Chron. 29; 2 Kings 22, 23.2; Chron. 34 and 35] *To procure the peace of the people,* as the same *David* saith [Psalms 72] *To decide all controversies that can arise among them* as *Salomon* did [I Kings 3]: *To be the Minister of God for the weale* [well-being] *of them that do well, and as the minister of God to take vengeance upon them that do evil,* as S. *Paul* saith [Romans 13]. And finally, *as a good Pastor, to go out and in before his people* as is said in the first of *Samuel: That through the Prince's Prosperity, the people's peace may be procured,* as *Jeremie* saith [Jeremiah 29].

And therefore in the Coronation of our own Kings, as well as of every Christian *Monarch* they give their Oath, first to maintain the Religion presently professed within their country, according to their laws, whereby it is established, and to punish all those that should press to alter, or disturb the profession thereof; And next to maintain all the...good Laws made by their predecessors; to see them put in execution, and the breakers and violators thereof, to be punished, according to the tenor of the same: and lastly, to maintain the whole country, and every state therein, in all their ancient Privileges and Liberties, as well against all foreign enemies, as among themselves: And shortly to procure the weale and flourishing of his people, not only in maintaining and putting to execution the old...law of the country, and by establishing of new (as necessity and evil manners will require) but by all other means possible to fore-see and prevent all dangers, that are likely to fall upon them, and to maintain concord, wealth, and civility among them, as a loving Father, and careful watchman, caring for them more than for himself, knowing himself to be ordained for them, and they not for him; and therefore countable to that great God, who placed him as his lieutenant over them, upon the peril of his soul to procure the weale of both souls and bodies, as far as in him lieth, of all them that are committed to his charge. And this oath in the Coronation is the clearest, civil, and fundamental Law, whereby the King's office is properly defined.

By the Law of Nature the King becomes the natural Father to all his Lieges at his Coronation: And as the Father of his fatherly duty is bound to care for the nourishing, education, and virtuous government of his children; even so is the king bound to care for all his subjects. As all the toil and pain that the father can take for his children, will be thought light and well bestowed by him, so that the effect thereof redound to their profit and weale; so ought the Prince to do towards his people. As the kindly father ought to foresee all inconveniences and dangers that may arise towards his children, and though with the hazard of his own person press to prevent the same; so ought the King towards his people. As the father's wrath and correction upon any of his children that offendeth, ought to be a fatherly chastisement seasoned with pity, as long as there is any hope of amendment in them; so ought the King towards any of his Lieges that offend in that measure. And shortly, as the Father's chief joy ought to be in procuring his children's welfare, rejoicing at their weale, sorrowing and pitying at their evil, to hazard for their safety, travel for their rest, wake for their sleep, and in a word, to think that his earthly felicity and life standeth and liveth more in them, nor in himself; so ought a good Prince think of his people. (54–6)

FROM *BASILICON DORON* (1599), IN *THE POLITICAL WORKS OF JAMES I*, ED. CHARLES HOWARD MCILWAIN

(Cambridge: Harvard University Press, 1918)

God gives not Kings the style of *Gods* in vain,
For on his Throne his Scepter do they sway:
And as their subjects ought them to obey,
So Kings should fear and serve their God again
If then ye would enjoy a happy reign,
Observe the Statutes of your heavenly King,
And from his Law, make all your Laws to spring:

Since his Lieutenant here ye should remain,
Reward the just, be steadfast, true, and plain,
Repress the proud, maintaining aye the right,
Walk always so, as ever in his sight,
Who guards the godly, plaguing the profane:
And so ye shall in Princely virtues shine,
Resembling right your mighty King Divine. (3)

A good King, thinking his highest honour to consist in the due discharge of his calling, employeth all his study and pains, to procure and maintain, by the making and execution of good Laws, the well-fare and peace of his people; and as their natural father and kindly Master, thinketh his greatest contentment standeth in their prosperity, and his greatest surety in having their hearts, subjecting his own private affections and appetites to the weale and standing of his Subjects, ever thinking common interest his chiefest particular: whereby the contrary, an usurping Tyrant, thinking his greatest honour and felicity to consist in attaining... to his ambitious pretenses, thinketh never himself sure, but by the dissension and factions among his people, and counterfeiting the Saint while he once creep in credit, will then (by inverting all good Laws to serve only for his unruly private affections) frame the common-weale ever to advance his particular: building his surety upon his people's misery: and in the end (as a step-father and an uncouth hireling) make up his own hand upon the ruins of the Republic. And according to their actions, so receive they their reward: For a good King (after a happy and famous reign) dieth in peace, lamented by his subjects, and admired by his neighbours; and leaving a reverent renown behind him in earth, obtaineth the Crown of eternal felicity in heaven. And although some of them (which falleth out very rarely) may be cut off by the treason of some unnatural subject, yet liveth their fame after them, and some notable plague faileth never to overtake the committers in this life, besides their infamy to all posterities hereafter: whereby the contrary, a Tyrant's miserable and infamous life, armeth in end his own Subjects to become his burreaux [hangman]: and although that rebellion be ever unlawfull on their part, yet is the world so wearied of him, that his fall is little meaned by the rest of his Subjects, and but smiled at by his neighbours. (18–19)

FROM KING JAMES I, A SPEECH TO THE LORDS AND COMMONS OF THE PARLIAMENT (MARCH 21, 1609), IN *THE POLITICAL WORKS OF JAMES I,* ED. CHARLES HOWARD MCILWAIN

(Cambridge: Harvard University Press, 1918)

The state of Monarchy is the supremest thing upon earth: For Kings are not only God's Lieutenants upon earth, and sit upon God's throne, but even by God himself they are called Gods. There be three principal similitudes that illustrate the state of Monarchy: One taken out of the word of God; and the two other out of the grounds of Policy and Philosophy. In the Scriptures Kings are called Gods, and so their power after a certain relation compared to the Divine power. Kings are also compared to Fathers of families: for a King is truly *Parens patriae,* the politique [political] father of his people. And lastly, Kings are compared to the head of the Microcosm of the body of man.

Kings are justly called Gods, for that they exercise a manner or resemblance of Divine power upon earth: For if you will consider the Attributes to God, you shall see how they agree in the person of a King. God hath power to create, or destroy, make, or unmake at his pleasure, to give life, or send death, to judge all, and to be judged nor accountable to none: To raise low things, and to make high things low at his pleasure, and to God are both soul and body due. And the like power have Kings: they make and unmake their subjects: They have power of raising, and casting down: of life, and of death: Judges over all their subjects, and in all causes, and yet accountable to none but God only. They have power to exalt low things, and abase high things, and make of their subjects like men at the Chess: A pawn to take a Bishop or a Knight, and to cry up or down any of their subjects, as they do their money. And to the King is due both the affection of the soul, and the service of the body of his subjects....

.... Now a Father may dispose of his Inheritance to his children, at his pleasure: yea, even disinherit the eldest upon just occasions, and prefer the youngest, according to his liking; make them beggars, or rich at his pleasure; restrain, or banish out of his presence, as he finds them give cause of offence, or restore them in favour again with the penitent sinner: So may the King deal with his Subjects.

And lastly, as for the head of the natural body, the head hath the power of directing all the members of the body to that use which the judgment in the head thinks most convenient. It may apply sharp cures, or cut off corrupt members, let blood in what proportion it thinks fit, and as the body may spare, but yet is all this power ordained by God *Ad aedificationem no ad destructionem* [for edification and not for destruction]. For although God have power as well of destruction, as of creation or maintenance; yet will it not agree with the wisdom of God to exercise his power in the destruction of nature, and overturning the whole frame of things, since his creatures were made, that his glory might thereby be the better expressed: So were he a foolish father that would disinherit or destroy his children without a cause, or leave off the careful education of them; And it were an idle head that would in place of physic so poison or phlebotomize the body as might breed a dangerous distemper or destruction thereof. (307–9)

THE UNION OF SCOTLAND AND ENGLAND

One of James's ambitions as king of both Scotland and England was to unite the two countries as one kingdom. He was not successful in attaining this goal as the English Parliament refused to agree to the union, but he continued to argue for the benefits of such a union for many years. The two documents that follow illustrate two of his attempts to persuade Parliament to support his efforts. The first of the two documents is an excerpt of James's first speech to the English Parliament after he became King of England. In this speech James lays out the advantages of a union between the two countries, noting that it will make them both stronger and richer, and he observes that since the two nations share one island, one language, and now one king, they seem to have been intended by God to be unified. Furthermore he compares himself as king to the head of a body, the husband of a wife, and the shepherd of a flock, and he asks his subjects to be merciful and not ask him to be the head of a divided body, the husband of two wives, or the shepherd of two flocks.

The second of the two documents is from James's speech to Parliament on March 31, 1607. In this speech James sounds less hopeful and more pleading. After four years as King of England, he is aware of the fears and doubts that keep the English Parliament from agreeing to the unification with Scotland. He therefore attempts to address each of these fears. The English, he knows, are concerned that he will be overly generous with the Scots, giving them all the benefit of the union and leaving all the work and sacrifice to the English. James, however, assures Parliament that he desires the equal good of both nations and that, as king, if he had wanted to favor Scotland he could have done so without their permission. James also knows that the English fear the poor Scots coming to England and taking their land and houses, but he reminds them that since there is more unused land in Scotland and more unemployed people in England, it would make more sense to send the idle English into Scotland. He admits that when he first became king he did spend a great deal, especially on his Scottish subjects, but he asserts that this was only because of his excitement over the new throne and because he did not want his Scottish subjects to think that he had forgotten them now that he was also the King of England. He assures the English Parliament that he has now rewarded all of the Scottish subjects who required rewarding, and that he will now spend less. Finally, he acknowledges the English concern about the depleting of the treasury, but he asserts that it is not too far depleted, that his liberal spending was justified as the king of two countries had to show his generosity to the subjects of two nations, and that he will soon increase the revenue of the Crown. He concludes by asking once again that the Parliament grant the union between the two countries, assuring them that he has the best interest of both nations at heart. In both speeches James speaks of the reunification of the kingdoms divided by King Lear, but in the second he sounds more like a penitent Lear, one who has learned to consider the welfare of his English subjects, of whom he has "taken too little care" (3.4.33–4).

FROM KING JAMES I, A SPEECH TO THE UPPER HOUSE OF PARLIAMENT (MONDAY, MARCH 19, 1603), IN *THE POLITICAL WORKS OF JAMES I,* ED. CHARLES HOWARD MCILWAIN

(Cambridge: Harvard University Press, 1918)

But although outward Peace be a great blessing; yet is it as far inferiour to peace within, as Civil wars are more cruel and unnatural than wars abroad. And therefore the second great blessing that God hath with my Person sent unto you, is Peace within, and that in a double form. First, by my descent lineally out of the loins of *Henry* the seventh, is reunited and confirmed in me the Union of the two Princely Roses of the two Houses of LANCASTER and YORKE.... But the Union of these two princely Houses, is nothing comparable to the Union of two ancient and famous Kingdoms, which is the other inward Peace annexed to my Person.

And here I must crave your patiences for a little space, to give me leave to discourse more particularly of the benefits that do arise of the Union which is made in my blood, being a matter that most properly belongeth to me to speak of, as the head wherein that great Body is united. And first, if we were to look not higher than to natural and Physical reasons, we may easily be persuaded of the great benefits that by that Union do redound to the whole Island: for if twenty thousand men be a strong Army, is not the double hereof, forty thousand, a double the stronger Army? If a Baron enricheth himself with double as many lands as he had before, is he not double the greater? Nature teacheth us, that Mountains are made of Motes, and that at the first, Kingdoms being divided, and every particular Towne or little County, as Tyrants or Usurpers could obtain the possession, a Segniorie apart, many of these little Kingdoms are now in process of time, by the ordinance of God, joined into great Monarchies, whereby they are become powerfull within themselves to defend themselves from all outward invasions, and their head and governor thereby enabled to redeem them from foreign assaults, and punish private transgressions within. Do we not yet remember, that this kingdom was divided into seven little Kingdoms, besides Wales? And is it not now the stronger by their union? And hath not the union of Wales to England added a greater strength thereto? Which though it was a great Principality, was nothing comparable in greatness and power to the ancient and famous Kingdom of Scotland. But what should we stick upon any natural appearance, when it is manifest that God by his Almighty providence hath preordained it so to be? Hath not God first united these two Kingdoms both in Language, Religion, and similitude of manners? Yea, hath he not made us all in one island, compassed with one Sea, and of it self by nature so indivisible as almost those that were borderers themselves on the late Borders, cannot distinguish, or know, or discern their own limits? These two Countries being separated neither by Sea, nor great River, Mountain, nor other strength of nature, but only by little small brooks, or demolished little walls, so as rather they were divided in apprehension, than in effect; And now in the end and fullness of time united, the right and title of both in my Person, alike lineally descended of both the Crowns whereby it is now become like a little World within it self, being entrenched and fortified round about with a natural, and yet admirable strong pond or ditch, whereby all the former fears of the Nation are now quite cut off: The other part of the Island being ever before now not only the place of landing to all strangers, that was to make invasion here, but likewise moved by the enemies of this State by untimely incursions, to make enforced diversion from their Conquests, for defending themselves at home, and keeping sure their back-door, as then it was called, which was the greatest hindrance and let that ever my Predecessors of this Nation gat in disturbing them from their many famous and glorious conquests abroad: What God hath conjoined then, let no man separate. I am the Husband, and all the whole Isle is my lawful Wife; I am the Head, and it is my Body; I am the Shepherd, and it is my flock: I hope therefore no man will be so unreasonable as to think that I that am a Christian King under the Gospel, should be a Polygamist and husband to two wives; that I being the Head, should have a divided and monstrous Body; or that being the Shepherd to so faire a Flock (whose fold hath no wall to hedge it but the four Seas) should have my Flock parted in two. But as I am assured, that no honest Subject of whatsoever degree within my whole dominions, is less glad of this joyful Union then I am; So may the frivolous objection of any that would be hinderers of this work, which God hath in my Person already established, be easily answered, which can be none, except such as are either blinded with Ignorance, or else transported with Malice, being unable to live in a well governed commonwealth, and only delighting to fish in troubled waters. For if they would stand upon their reputation and privileges of any of the Kingdoms, I pray you was not both the Kingdoms Monarchies from the beginning, and consequently could ever the Body be counted without the Head, which was ever inseparably joined thereunto? So that as Honour and Privileges of any of the Kingdoms could not be divided from their Sovereign; So are they now confounded & joined in my Person, who am equal and alike kindly Head to you both. When this Kingdom of England was divided into so many little Kingdoms as I told you before; one of them behooved to eat up another, till they were all united in one. And yet can *Wiltsire* or *Devonshire,* which were of the *West Saxons,* although their Kingdom was of longest durance, and did by conquest overcome divers of the rest of the little Kingdoms, make claim to Priority of Place of Honour before *Sussex, Essex,* or other Shires which were conquered by them? And have we not the like experience in the Kingdome of *France,* being composed of divers Dutchies, and one after another conquered by the sword? For even as little brooks lose their names by their running and fall into great Rivers, and the very name and memory of the great Rivers swallowed up in the Ocean: so by the conjunction of divers little Kingdoms in one, are all these private differences and questions swallowed up.... And as God hath made *Scotland* the one half of this Isle to enjoy my Birth, and the first and most imperfect half of my life, and you here to enjoy the perfect and the last half thereof; so can I not think that any would be so injurious to me, no not in their thoughts and wishes, as to cut asunder the one half of me from the other. But in this matter I have far enough insisted, resting assured that in your hearts and minds you all applaud this my discourse. (271–3)

FROM KING JAMES I, A SPEECH TO BOTH HOUSES OF PARLIAMENT (MARCH 31, 1607), IN *THE POLITICAL WORKS OF JAMES I,* ED. CHARLES HOWARD MCILWAIN

(Cambridge: Harvard University Press, 1918)

For the first, what I crave, I protest before God who knows my heart, and to you my people before whom it were a shame to lie, that I claim nothing but with acknowledgement of my Bond to you; that as ye owe to me subjection and obedience: So my Sovereignty obligeth me to yield to you love, government and protection: Neither did I ever wish any happiness to my self, which was not conjoined with the happiness of my people. I desire a perfect Union of Laws and persons, and such a Naturalizing as may make one body of both Kingdoms under me your King, That I and my posterity (if it so please God) may rule over you to the world's end; Such an union as was of the Scots and Pictes in Scotland, and of the Heptarchie here in England. And for Scotland I avow such an Union, as if you had got it by Conquest, but such a Conquest as may be cemented by love, the only sure bond of subjection or friendship....For no more possible is it for one King to govern two Countries *Contiguous,* the one a great, the other a less, a richer and a poorer, the greater drawing like an Adamant the lesser to the Commodities thereof, than for one head to govern two bodies, or one man to be husband of two wives....

But what preparation is it which I crave? Only such as by the entrance may show something is done, yet more is intended. There is a conceit entertained, and a double jealousy possesseth many, wherein I am misjudged.

First, that this Union will be the *Crisis* to the overthrow of England, and setting up of Scotland: England will then be overwhelmed by the swarming of the Scots, who if the Union were effected, would reign and rule all.

The second is, my profuse liberality to the Scottish men more than the English, and that with this Union all things shall be given to them, and you turned out of all: To you shall be left the sweat and labour, to them shall be given the fruit and sweet: and that my forbearance is but till this Union may be gained. How agreeable is this to the truth, Judge you; And that not by my words, but by my Actions. Do I crave the Union without exceptions? Do I not offer to bind my self and to reserve to you, as in the Instrument, all places of Judicature? Do I intend any thing which standeth not with the equal good of both Nations? I could then have done it, and not spoken of it: For all men of understanding must agree, that I might dispose without assent of Parliament, Offices of Judicature, and others, both Ecclesiastical and Temporal: But herein I did voluntarily offer by my Letters from Royston to the Commissioners, to bind my Prerogative.

Some think that I will draw the Scottish Nation hither, talking idly of transporting of Trees out of a barren ground into a better, and of lean cattle out of bad pasture into a more fertile soil. Can any man displant you, unless you will? Or can any man think that Scotland is so strong to pull you out of your houses? Or do you not think I know England hath more people, Scotland more waste ground? So that there is room in Scotland rather to plant your idle people that swarm in London Streets, and other Towns, and disburden you of them, than to bring more unto you; And in cases of Justice if I be partial to either side, let my own mouth condemn me, as unworthy to be your King.

I appeal to your selves, if in favour of Justice I have been partial: Nay, my intention was ever, you should then have most cause to praise my discretion, when you saw I had most power. If hitherto I have done nothing to your prejudice, much less mean I hereafter. If when I might have done it without any breach of promise; Think so of me, that much less I will do it, when a Law is to restrain me. I owe no more to Scottish men than to the English. I was borne there, and sworn here, and now reign over both. Such particular persons of the Scottish Nation, as might claim any extraordinary merit at my hands, I have already reasonably rewarded, and I can assure you that there is none left, whom for I mean extraordinary to strain myself further, than in such ordinary benefit as I may equal bestow without mine own great hurt, upon any Subject of either Nation; In which case no King's hands can ever be fully closed. To both I owe Justice and protection, which with God's grace I shall ever equally balance.

For my Liberality, I have told you of it heretofore: my three first years were to me as a Christmas, I could not then be miserable: should I have been oversparing to them? They might have thought *Joseph* had forgotten his brethren, or that the King had been drunk with his new Kingdome. But Suits go not now so cheap as they were wont, neither are there so many fees taken in the Hamper and Pettibag for the great Seal as hath been. And if I did respect the English when I came first, of whom I was received with joy, and came as in a hunting journey, what might the Scottish have justly said, if I had not in some measure dealt bountifully with them that so long had served me, so far adventured themselves with me, and been so faithful to me. I have given you now four years proof since my coming, and what I might have done more to have raised the Scottish nation you all now, and the longer I live the less cause have I to be acquainted with them, and so the less hope of extraordinary favour towards them: For since my coming from them I do not already know the one half of them by face, most of the youth being now risen up to be men, who were but children when I was there, and more are borne since my coming thence.

Now for my lands and revenues of the Crown which you may think I have diminished, They are not yet so far diminished, but that I think no prince of Christendom hath fairer possessions to his Crown than yet I have: and in token of my care to preserve the same to my posterity for ever, the entail of my lands to the Crown hath been long ago offered unto you: and that it is not yet done is not my fault as you know. My Treasurer here knoweth my care and hath already in part declared it, and if I did not hope to treble my Revenue more then I have impaired it, I should never rest quietly in my bed. But notwithstanding my coming to the Crown with that extraordinary applause which you all know, and that I had two Nations to be the objects of my liberality, which never any Prince had here before; will you compare my gifts out of mine inheritance with some Princes here that had only this Nation to respect, and whose whole time of reign was little longer than mine, albeit as I have already said, they had nothing so great cause of using their liberality. . . .

Now to conclude, I am glad of this occasion. . . . You are now to recede: when you meet again, remember I pray you, the truth and sincerity of my meaning, which in seeking Union, is only to advance the greatness of your Empire seated here in England; And yet with such caution I wish it, as may stand with the weale of both States. What is now desired, hath oft before been sought when it could not be obtained: To refuse it now then, were double iniquity. Strengthen your own felicity, *London* must be the Seat of your King, and Scotland joined to this kingdom by a Golden conquest, but cemented with love, (as I said before) which within will make you strong against all Civil and intestine Rebellion, as without we will be compassed and guarded with our walls of brass. Judge me charitably, since in this I seek your equal good, that so both of you might be made fearful to your Enemies, powerful in your selves, and available to your friends. Study therefore hereafter to make a good Conclusion, avoid all delays, cut off all vain questions, that your King may have his lawful desire, and be not disgraced in his just ends. And for your security in such reasonable points of restrictions, whereunto I am to agree, ye need never doubt of my inclination: For I will not say anything which I will not promise, nor promise any thing which I will not swear; What I swear I will sign, and what I sign, I shall with God's grace ever perform. (292–6; 304–5)

KING JAMES ACCORDING TO HIS CONTEMPORARIES

The last four documents in this chapter were written not by James himself but rather by his contemporaries, and they reveal how some people viewed James during his lifetime. The first document is a journal entry written by a subject of Queen Elizabeth I and King James I. Sir Roger Wilbraham here records the death of Queen Elizabeth and the succession to the throne of King James. Wilbraham notes the great relief everyone felt at the smooth transition of power and the initially positive reception of the King. As we see in the final scene of *King Lear,* the lack of a clear heir to take the throne can be very troubling for a kingdom, and so naturally the English people were pleased to have a king and a trouble-free transition. But Wilbraham also notes how many men James knighted in his journey to London, how many appealed to the new king to give them some favor, and how many received that favor. Even early on, it seems, James was demonstrating some of the controversial behavior that will be alluded to in *King Lear.*

FROM SIR ROGER WILBRAHAM, *THE JOURNAL OF SIR ROGER WILBRAHAM,* IN *THE JOURNAL OF SIR ROGER WILBRAHAM* (1513–1616), TOGETHER WITH NOTES IN ANOTHER HAND (1642–1649), ED. HAROLD SPENCER SCOTT

(London: Offices of the Royal Historical Society, 1902)

March 20, 1603

... and it pleased God to give such time of preparation & expectation of her [Queen Elizabeth's] death, that she dying the Thursday after midnight, at 9 of the clock in the morn, the council & lords had assembled themselves at Whitehall (coming from Richmond) & there the 24 of March within 8 hours after the Queen's death subscribed the Proclamation with 30 hands at least, & then [instantly] proclaimed the Queen's death, & the true and rightful succession of King James the first king of England, of Scotland James the sixth. Whereupon the people both in city & counties finding the just fear of 40 years, for want of a known successor, dissolved in a minute did so rejoice, as few wished the gracious Queen alive again, but as the world is... inclined to alteration of government, both papists and protestants, as it seemed, many having discontentment in their private opinions though perhaps none in truth, & more hoping to be bettered by the succeeding king, in whose virtues & prudence there is admirable expectation. God for his mercy grant the wealth of England, & the flattery of the

A SPENDTHRIFT KING

The following document is from Francis Osborne's *Some Traditional Memoirs on the Reign of King James the First.* In this excerpt of his memoirs Osborne recounts a story that reveals James's spendthrift nature. James, it seems, was in the habit of giving away great quantities of money to his favorites without realizing how much he was giving away. When he actually saw the money or had it in his possession, however, he was much less willing to part with it. Thus Robert Cecil, who was himself said to have sometimes encouraged the King to spend large amounts of money, here attempts to prevent James from giving an extremely generous gift to one of his favorites by piling the money in a room through which James was to pass so that he would see it before relinquishing it.

While we never see King Lear giving away vast sums of money, we do see him foolishly giving away his kingdom without having considered the consequences of his actions. We also hear him express his regret about having neglected the poor while enjoying the "pomp" and "superflux" of the kingdom (3.4.34, 36). If *King Lear* makes reference to some of King James's pet projects, it also makes reference to some of the weaknesses that his subjects perceived in him.

FROM FRANCIS OSBORNE, ESQ., *SOME TRADITIONAL MEMOIRS ON THE REIGN OF KING JAMES I* (1658), IN *THE SECRET HISTORY OF THE COURT OF JAMES THE FIRST*, VOL. 1

(Edinburgh: James Ballantyne and Co, 1811)

In this place, my memory presents me with Sir Robert Cecil, after Earl of Salisbury, famed for the most mortal enemy of the Earl of Essex, and a seducer of the king, by persuading him this nation was so rich, it could be neither exhausted nor provoked: a saying generally laid to his charge, yet contradicted in this practice of his; for the Earle of Sommerset, being in the flower of his favour before he had either wife or beard, had got a peremptory warrant to the treasurer for 20,000ls.; who, in his exquisite prudence, finding, that not only the exchequer, but the Indies themselves, would in time want fluency to feed so immense a prodigality, and not without reason apprehending the king as ignorant in the value of what was demanded, as the desert of the person that begged it, and knowing a pound, upon the Scotch account, would not pay for the shooing of a horse, by which his master might be farther led out of the way of thrift, than in his own nature he was willing to go, being observed very tenacious in the distribution of any money passed through his hands or in his presence; laid the former-mentioned sum upon this ground in a room through which his majesty was to pass: who, amazed at the quantity, as a sight not unpossibly his eyes never saw before, asked the treasurer whose money it was, who answered, Yours, before you gave it away; whereupon the king fell into passion, protesting he was abused, never intending any such gift: and casting himself upon the heap, scrabled out the quantity of two or three hundred pounds, and swore he should have no more. (231–3)

THE KING'S DETRACTORS

Sir Anthony Weldon's *The Character of King James* paints a rather unflattering portrait of the king, noting not only his mismanaging of money and his fickleness with his favorites, but also observing many physical defects. Weldon's critical portrayal of the king may have been due in part to his dismissal from a court office when a satirical pamphlet he had written about Scotland was discovered. Weldon, resenting this dismissal, became very critical of the king. Nevertheless, several of his criticisms were voiced by others as well, and thus Weldon's work does show how at least one segment of the kingdom perceived James. As you read, note which of Weldon's comments are echoed by others and which are contradicted by other documents in this chapter. Consider, also, what sort of criticisms one of Lear's subjects might have made of Lear. In what ways does Anthony Weldon's portrayal of King James resemble King Lear?

FROM SIR ANTHONY WELDON, *THE CHARACTER OF KING JAMES* (1650), IN *THE SECRET HISTORY OF THE COURT OF JAMES THE FIRST*, VOL. 2

(Edinburgh: James Ballantyne and Co, 1811)

This king's character is much easier to take than his picture, for he could never be brought to sit for the taking of that, which is the reason of so few good pieces of him; but his character was obvious to every eye.

He was of a middle stature, more corpulent through his clothes than in his body, yet fat enough, his clothes ever being made large and easy, the doublets quilted for stiletto proof, his breeches in great pleats and full stuffed; he was naturally of a timorous disposition, which was the reason of his quilted doublets; his eyes large, ever rolling after any stranger that came in his presence, insomuch, as many for shame have left the room, as being out of countenance; his beard was very thin: his tongue too large for his mouth, which ever made him speak full in the mouth, and made him drink very uncomely, as if eating his drink, which came out into the cup of each side of his mouth; his skin as soft as taffeta sarsnet, which felt so, because he never washed his hands, only rubbed his fingers' ends slightly with the wet end of a napkin; his legs were very weak, having had (as was thought) some foul play in his youth, or rather before he was born, that he was not able to stand at seven years of age, that weakness made him ever leaning on other men's shoulders; his walk was ever circular, his fingers ever in that walk fiddling bout his cod-piece; he was very temperate in his exercises and in his diet, and not intemperate in his drinking.... he was very constant in all things, (his favorites excepted,) in which he loved change, yet never cast down any (he once raised) from the height of greatness, though from their wonted nearness and privacy; unless by their own default, by opposing his change.... In his diet, apparel, and journeys, he was very constant; in his apparel so constant, as by his good will he would never change his clothes until worn out to very rags....

He was very witty, and had as many ready witty jests as any man living, at which he would not smile himself, but deliver them in a grave and serious manner. He was very liberal of what he had not in his own gripe, and would rather part with 100 li. he never had in his keeping then one twenty shilling piece within his own custody; he spent much, and had much use of his subjects' purses, which bred some clashings with them in parliament; yet would always come off, and end with a sweet and plausible close; and truly his bounty was not discommendable, for his raising favourites was the worst; rewarding old servants, and relieving his native countrymen, was infinitely more to be commended in him than condemned. His sending ambassadors were no less chargeable then dishonourable and unprofitable to him and his whole kingdom; for he was ever abused in all negotiations, yet he had rather spend 100,000 li. On embassies, to keep or procure peace with dishonour, then 10,000 li. on an army that would have forced peace with honour....

He was very crafty and cunning in petty things, as the circumventing any great man, the change of a favourite, etc. insomuch, as a very wise man was wont to say, he believed him the wisest fool in Christendom, meaning him wise in small things, but a fool in weighty affaires.

He ever desired to prefer mean men in great places, that when he turned them out again, they should have no friend to bandy with them: And besides, they were so hated by being raised from a mean estate, to overtop all men, that every one held it a pretty recreation to have them often turned out: There were living in this king's time, at one instant, two treasurers, three secretaries, two lord keepers, two admirals, three lord chief justices, yet but one in play, therefore this king had a pretty faculty in putting out and in. By this you may perceive in what his wisdom consisted, but in great and weighty affaires ever at his wits end....

In a word, he was (take him altogether and not in pieces) such a king, I wish this kingdom have never any worse, on the condition, not any better; for he lived in peace, died in peace, and left all his kingdoms in a peaceable condition.... (1–12)

THE VIEW FROM ABROAD

The following document shows how James I was perceived by a foreign am‐
bassador to England. Molin certainly portrays James's physical appearance in
a more flattering light than Weldon did, and he also credits James with great
intelligence. He also, however, notes many of the complaints that James's sub‐
jects made about him, including his hatred of crowds, his great love of the
hunt and his willingness to leave the government of the kingdom to others
while he enjoyed this pastime, and his avoidance of war. Molin also observes
that Prince Henry, though not as intellectual as his father, seemed to have a
better understanding of what the English people desired in a king. As you read
this passage, consider what a foreign ambassador might have said about Lear
and about his relationships with his subjects and with his children.

FROM NICOLO MOLIN, REPORT ON ENGLAND
PRESENTED TO THE GOVERNMENT OF VENICE (1607), IN
*CALENDAR OF STATE PAPERS AND MANUSCRIPTS RELATING
TO ENGLISH AFFAIRS, EXISTING IN THE ARCHIVES AND
COLLECTIONS OF VENICE,* VOL. 10, 1603–1607

(London: Kraus Reprint, 1970)

So then King James VI of Scotland and I of England is now on the throne. He was
born in 1563, and will complete his forty third year on the 19th of this month. He is
sufficiently tall, of a noble presence, his physical constitution robust, and he is at pains
to preserve it by taking much exercise at the chase [hunt], which he passionately loves,
and uses not only as a recreation, but as a medicine. For this he throws off all busi‐
ness, which he leaves to his Council and to his Ministers. And so one may truly say
that he is Sovereign in name and in appearance rather than in substance and effect.
This is the result of his deliberate choice, for he is capable of governing, being a Prince
of intelligence and culture above the common, thanks to his application to and plea‐
sure in study when he was young, though he has now abandoned that pursuit alto‐
gether. He is a Protestant, as it is called; that means a mixture of a number of religions;
in doctrine he is Calvinistic, but not so in politics and in policy; for Calvin denies au‐
thority not merely spiritual but temporal as well, a doctrine that will always be ab‐
horred by every Sovereign.... (510–11)
His Majesty is by nature placid, averse from cruelty, a lover of justice. He goes to
chapel on Sundays and Tuesdays, the latter being observed by him in memory of his
escape from a conspiracy of Scottish nobles in 1600. He loves quiet and repose, has

not inclination to war, nay is opposed to it, a fact that little pleases many of his subjects, though it pleases them still less that he leaves all government to his Council and will think of nothing but the chase. He does not caress the people nor make them that good cheer the late Queen did, whereby she won their loves; for the English adore their Sovereigns, and if the King passed through the same street a hundred times a day the people would still run to see him; they like their King to show pleasure at their devotion, as the late Queen knew well how to do; but this King manifests no taste for them but rather contempt and dislike. The result is he is despised and almost hated. In fact his Majesty is more inclined to live retired with eight or ten of his favourites than openly, as is the custom of the country and the desire of the people.…

By this marriage [to Queen Anne] the King has had four children, two boys and two girls. The eldest, Henry, is about twelve years old, of a noble wit and great promise. His every action is marked by a gravity most certainly beyond his years. He studies, but not with much delight, and chiefly under his father's spur, not of his own desire, and for this he is often admonished and set down. Indeed one day the King, after giving him a lecture, said that if he did not attend more earnestly to his lessons the crown would be left to his brother, the Duke of York, who was far quicker at learning and studies more earnestly. The Prince made no reply, out of respect for his father: but when he went to his room and his tutor continued in the same vein, he said, "I know what becomes a Prince. It is not necessary for me to be a professor, but a soldier and a man of the world. If my brother is as learned as they say, we'll make him Archbishop of Canterbury." The King took this answer in no good part; nor is he overpleased to see his son so beloved and of such promise that his subjects place all their hopes in him; and it would almost seem, to speak quite frankly that the King was growing jealous; and so the Prince has great need of a wise counselor to guide his steps.…

I have remarked that his Majesty is devoted to the chase and to his pleasure, and hates all the trouble and anxiety of Government. He readily leaves all to the Council.…

The Council usually follows the King unless he goes privately on a party of pleasure, and then it stays with the Court ordinarily in London. Their power is great, nay excessively great; not that they have it of right, but because they have slowly usurped it. It was never greater than now, thanks to the indulgence and carelessness of the King. Though divided among themselves upon many points they are united on this, to preserve their authority, which they use not merely to aggrandize but to enrich themselves as well.… (513–4)

QUESTIONS FOR WRITTEN AND ORAL DISCUSSION

1. Read the excerpt from *Basilicon Doron* and consider Lear's character in light of this document. Would James have considered Lear a good king, a tyrant, or some combination of the two? What is your opinion of Lear?

2. Imagine that you and your classmates are members of the English Parliament during the reign of James I. You have heard James's parliamentary speeches, and you have

seen *King Lear.* Would you vote for the unification of Scotland and England? Hold debates, with some students arguing for the unification and some arguing against it. You may use evidence from the documents in this chapter and from *King Lear.*

3. In his books and speeches James I describes his vision of what a king should be. What characteristics do you think a ruler should have? Does Lear embody these characteristics? Would any of the characters in *King Lear* be the type of ruler you would want to rule your country?

4. Imagine that you are one of Lear's subjects and write an account of Lear. What is he like as a king? What does he look like, how does he act, and what are his strengths and weaknesses? Would your account resemble Sir Anthony Weldon's portrayal of King James?

5. How does your account of Lear (in question #4, above) compare with the accounts of James in this chapter?

6. Compare the Venetian ambassador's opinion of James with the opinions of his subjects. Who portrays him more favorably? Do you think the same would be true for Lear?

7. What would the King of France, or another foreign ambassador, have said about Lear? Would a foreign ambassador's portrayal of Lear resemble Nicolo Molin's account of King James? What criticisms or praise would be similar? What would be different?

8. In what ways does Lear seem to be similar to James? In what ways are they different? Do you think James would have found the similarities offensive or flattering?

9. James compares kings to fathers. Overall, is Lear a good father to his subjects? At what points is he a good father to his subjects and at what points does he fail to be a good father?

SUGGESTED READINGS

Akrigg, G.P.V. *Jacobean Pageant or The Court of King James I.* Cambridge, MA: Harvard U P, 1962.

Ashton, Robert, ed. *James I By His Contemporaries.* London: Hutchinson & Co., 1969.

Bergeron, David M. *Royal Family, Royal Lovers: King James of England and Scotland.* Columbia, MO and London: U of Missouri P, 1991.

Kernan, Alvin B. *Shakespeare: The King's Playwright: Theater in the Stuart Court, 1603–1613.* New Haven, CT: Yale UP, 1995.

4

"According to my bond": Family Ties in Shakespeare's Time

King Lear continues to appeal to modern readers and audiences in part because it is not only a play about kings, kingdoms, and politics, but also a play about families and family responsibilities. While few contemporary readers have ever had to rule or divide a kingdom, most of us can understand that the complex relationships between parents and children contain the material for great drama, and great tragedy. Love for our family members may inspire us to acts of loyalty and even to heroic gestures such as those made by Cordelia and Edgar, but we may also feel resentment and anger towards those family members who have mistreated us or who have not behaved as we expected.

Our familiarity with family relationships, however, may itself mislead us. While families in Shakespeare's time shared many similarities with families in our own time, they also differed from our families in some important ways. In order to better understand what Cordelia means when she says that she loves her father "according to [her] bond," we need to understand what bonds united families in Shakespeare's time.

It should first be observed that families in Shakespeare's day, like families in our own time, cannot be easily and simply classified. Family dynamics and family structures varied from one family to another, just as they do now, and economic matters like inheritance and marriage arrangements differed greatly depending on the social and economic status of the family. The issue of inheritance, which was so crucial to the families of Lear and Gloucester, would not have had so great an effect on poorer families with little or no property to pass on to the next generation.

Furthermore, though the behavior and the duties of individual family members were described in early modern literature as well as in sermons and conduct books (manuals describing the appropriate behavior of each family member) not all families followed these manuals and sermons or behaved in the way families were portrayed on stage or in literature. Just as the families that we see on television or in the movies may not always resemble our own families, so the familial roles laid out in conduct books or described in the literature of the day may not have always been followed by actual families. Nevertheless, examining the roles that sermons and conduct books prescribed for families in Shakespeare's time and the behavior that Shakespeare and others portrayed on the page and on the stage allows us to better understand what was expected of family members in the seventeenth century and to learn what issues caused problems for early modern families and thus raised the concern of writers and preachers. This chapter includes excerpts from sermons, conduct manuals, legal treatises, and plays. In most cases the spelling and punctuation have been modernized for the sake of clarity.

PATRIARCHY AND PRIMOGENITURE

In general, families in Shakespeare's England were patriarchal and followed the custom of primogeniture. In a patriarchy the family is governed by the father or by the oldest living male in the family. Primogeniture means that the eldest son inherits all or most of the property, with perhaps smaller amounts of money or land being provided for daughters and younger sons. Ideally the daughters would be given a dowry, which would allow them to marry well, and younger sons would be given an education, which would prepare them to make a living. The practice of primogeniture was designed to protect the family property and to keep it from being divided (as Lear's kingdom was) into smaller and smaller portions with each passing generation. One large estate passed from father to eldest son and maintained intact was more valuable than several small estates, which might be divided into still smaller estates until no member of the family had enough property or land to live on. The system, however, was not without its flaws. Not all families had enough money or property to provide dowries and educations for their daughters and younger sons, and even the eldest son was limited by primogeniture, since he had to wait for the death of his father before he could inherit the estate. This is what is alluded to in the letter supposedly written by Edgar but really forged by Edmund:

> This policy and reverence of age makes the world bitter to the best of our times; keeps our fortunes from us till our oldness cannot relish them. I begin to find

an idle and fond bondage in the oppression of aged tyranny; who sways, not as it has power, but as it is suffered. Come to me, that of this I may speak more. If our father would sleep till I waked him, you should enjoy half his revenue for ever, and live the beloved of your brother, Edgar. (1.2.45–52)

This letter is supposedly Edgar voicing his complaint about having to wait for his old and foolish father to die before he can inherit, and promising Edmund half of his inheritance if he would help Edgar to murder their father. In reality, of course, the letter is planted by Edmund to turn Gloucester against Edgar, and it is Edmund, not Edgar, who wants to overturn the custom of primogeniture.

DAUGHTERS AND DOWRIES

The practice of primogeniture generally excluded daughters from inheriting the bulk of the estate, although in some families daughters did inherit some property even when they had brothers. In families without sons, daughters might be made co-heirs, and the land and money might be divided between them. The land might also pass to another male relative, or it might be passed to the eldest daughter. The latter was the case in the royal Tudor family. King Henry VIII declared that after his death his son Edward would rule, followed by Mary, his eldest daughter, and then Elizabeth. For most daughters, however, their primary source of financial security was in marriage. When the daughter of a wealthy or property-holding family was to be married, her family would provide her and her groom with a dowry. This dowry, which might consist of both property and cash, would help the newly married couple to live more comfortably, and it might also help to attract a better husband for the daughter. This explains why, in the first scene of *King Lear,* the Duke of Burgundy, who has been pursuing a marriage with Cordelia, withdraws his suit upon learning that Lear will not give her a dowry. A woman of Cordelia's class without any dowry would have little chance of marrying well, since her future husband would have no financial incentive to marry her and no financial security if he did marry her. The groom's family also provided money, known as the jointure, for the bride to live on if the groom died before her. The dowry therefore helped to secure both a husband and a jointure so that the bride would be provided for both during and after her marriage. Thus Cordelia, disinherited by her father as she is on the brink of marriage, is left without any financial security. She has no dowry with which to attract a husband, and no jointure on which to live without one. She is, in fact, "dowered with [Lear's] curse" (1.1.205), and any man who married her would be risking the king's disapproval. Fortunately for her, the King of France can see that "she is herself a dowry" (1.1.242). Without such a husband, Lear's "dowerless daughter" would be utterly destitute (1.1.257).

The fact that Cordelia is a daughter about to be married, moreover, considerably complicates her situation at the beginning of the play. Marriage, and the wedding ceremony, would require her to pledge her love, obedience, and honor to her husband. Love, honor, and obedience have also been what she, as a dutiful daughter, owed to her parents. Upon marriage she will have what Desdemona in *Othello* describes as "a divided duty" (1.3.180). She will owe love, honor, and obedience to both father and husband, though biblical sources, Renaissance sermons, and conduct books all suggest that after marriage her primary duty will be to her husband, with whom she will become one person, and who will in some sense take the place of her father and family. Yet Lear is asking her, as he asked her sisters, to pledge all her love to him. He is not satisfied with receiving "half [her] love...half [her] care and duty" while her husband receives the other half (1.1.101). He forces Cordelia to choose between making a pledge to him that would then make her wedding vows a lie and relinquishing the dowry that will make her marriage possible.

ILLEGITIMATE CHILDREN

Illegitimate children, or children born outside of a marriage, were generally excluded from the system of inheritance and primogeniture, though there were loopholes in the laws that would at times allow them to inherit. Technically an illegitimate child was not legally recognized as the father's child. He was not "a son by the order of law" as Gloucester says that Edgar, his legitimate son, is (1.1.18), and therefore Edmund, his illegitimate son, could not inherit his father's estate. Ecclesiastical law, or church law, however, allowed fathers to leave their illegitimate children enough money or property to maintain, feed, clothe, and educate them, and even to provide money so that they could marry well. This was probably in part because of the financial concerns otherwise raised by bastard children. If a child were born to an unwed mother and the father could not be found or would not acknowledge the child, then the child would often "fall on the parish." That is, the child became the financial responsibility of the parish, or the community in which he lived. He would be supported by the parish and would be a financial drain on the parish until he was old enough to be apprenticed or otherwise put to work. In order to prevent such economic burdens, every effort was made to determine the father of the child. When an unmarried woman went into labor, the midwife would be instructed to ask the woman, when she was in her greatest labor pains, to name the father. It was thought that at these moments of great pain she was likely to tell the truth. If a father could be found, or if he willingly acknowledged the child, then he might be held financially responsible for the child. Gloucester seems to have acknowledged and taken financial responsibility for his illegitimate son, Edmund. When Kent asks Gloucester if Edmund is his son, Gloucester replies: "His breeding, sir, hath been at my charge. I have so often blushed to acknowledge him, that now I am brazed to it" (1.1.8–10). Gloucester's answer is legally accurate. Legally Edmund is not his son, but his "breeding" has been at Gloucester's "charge" in two senses: he fathered him, and he has paid for his upbringing. Gloucester has supported him, admitting that "the whoreson must be acknowledged" (1.1.20), and though Edmund is both illegitimate and younger than Edgar, Gloucester claims that his eldest, legitimate son is "no dearer in my account" (1.1.19), another phrase that can suggest both an emotional and a financial tie. Edmund is just as dear, or just as beloved, as Edgar, but he is also just as dear, or just as expensive, in Gloucester's financial accounts.

THE EMOTIONAL BONDS OF PARENTS AND CHILDREN

Family relations, of course, were not simply economic. Bonds of love, loyalty, and duty also tied together those living in one household. Conduct books, sermons, and the Bible all gave instructions on how parents and children were supposed to treat each other. Parents were supposed to love their children and to provide for the physical needs of their children, feeding, clothing, and sheltering them. They were also supposed to educate their children; instruct them in the Christian, protestant faith; prepare them for a career; and arrange for them to marry as well as possible. Children were to love, honor, and obey their parents. Daughters, in particular, were to be silent and obedient, not questioning their parents' decisions. When their parents became old, or if they grew sick and weak, the children were supposed to care for them, providing whatever they needed and continuing to respect and honor them.

MASTERS AND SERVANTS

A Renaissance household did not merely contain parents and their children. Servants were considered part of the household, if not exactly part of the family, and conduct manuals also delineated the roles of both master and servant. Masters were in charge of their servants, but they were instructed to remember that they were themselves servants of God. They were to supervise their servants and make sure that they attended church and were not engaged in dangerous or immoral activities. Servants were to serve their masters loyally, as they would serve God. Even when a master commanded them to do something they thought unreasonable, they were to obey without questioning. The only exception to this rule was if the master asked the servant to do something that would be wrong in God's eyes. In that case the servant was to choose to follow God rather than the master. The familial relationships between masters and servants are also important in *King Lear*. Kent risks banishment and his master's fury by speaking the truth to Lear and doing what he knows is right. He compares the relationship of master and servant to that of father and son, calling Lear "Royal Lear, / Whom I have ever honored as my king, / Loved as my father, as my master followed" (1.1.139–41). It is because of these bonds of duty between master and servant that Kent will risk everything to serve his master as he feels he must, and similar bonds will cause Cornwall's servant to sacrifice his life in an attempt to keep his master from doing evil.

SHAKESPEARE'S FATHERS AND DAUGHTERS

Many of Shakespeare's plays feature father-daughter relationships, and several particularly focus on the pressures put on that relationship when daughters, like Cordelia, are on the brink of marriage. Desdemona, like Cordelia, acknowledges her bond to her father and her duty to repay him for her "life and education" with her duty and obedience. Nevertheless, she reminds him that she, like her mother before her, has come to a time in life when she must owe more duty to her husband than to her father. Hermia, in *A Midsummer Night's Dream,* is reminded that her father should be obeyed as a god and that he has the power to have her killed if she does not obey him. Yet she persists in eloping with the man she loves rather than marrying the man her father has chosen for her. The Duke in *The Two Gentlemen of Verona* pretends that he, like Lear, is prepared to disown his daughter, cast her out, and give her no dowry, though he does this only to trick her lover into betraying their plans to elope. The portrayal of such father-daughter dilemmas in Shakespeare's plays reveals the delicacy of this particular point in the relationship. The daughter's duty pulls her in two directions at once. As a daughter, she should obey her father in all things, but as a woman about to be married she is preparing to join herself with another man to whom she will owe her love, honor, and obedience, and she wishes to have some part in choosing that man. The father, meanwhile, has cared for, controlled, and made decisions for his daughter all of her life, and it is difficult for him to admit that this period of fatherly dominion is over and that he is getting older and moving into a stage of life in which he will not be the central man in his daughter's world and will not be in control of her decisions. Giving his daughter away in marriage requires him to give up his close relationship to his daughter and to give up his position of prominence in her life.

All of the texts below are taken from the *Illustrated Sterling Edition of Shakespeare's Works.* Boston: Dana Estes & Co., 1901. 10 vols. 1900–01.

FROM *OTHELLO*

Brabantio: I pray you hear her speak;
If she confess that she was half the wooer,
Destruction on my head if my bad blame
Light on the man!—Come hither, gentle mistress;
Do you perceive in all this noble company
Where most you owe obedience?

Desdemona: My noble father,
I do perceive here a divided duty.
To you I am bound for life and education;
My life and education both do learn me
How to respect you; You are the lord of duty,
I am hitherto your daughter; But here's my husband,
And so much duty as my mother showed
To you, preferring you before her father,
So much I challenge that I may profess
Due to the Moor my Lord.

Brabantio: God be with you! I have done.—
Please it your grace, on to the state affairs:
I had rather to adopt a child than get it.
Come hither, Moor.
I here do give thee that with all my heart,
Which, but thou hast already, with all my heart
I would keep from thee. [To Desdemona]—For your sake, jewel,
I am glad at soul I have no other child;
For thy escape would teach me tyranny,
To hang clogs on 'em.—I have done, my lord. (Vol. 9; 1.3.175–198)

FROM *A MIDSUMMER NIGHT'S DREAM*

Egeus: I beg the ancient privilege of Athens,
As she is mine, I may dispose of her,
Which shall be either to this gentleman
Or to her death, according to our law
Immediately provided in that case.

Theseus: What say you, Hermia? Be advised, fair maid:
To you your father should be as a god;
One that composed your beauties; yea, and one
To whom you are but as a form in wax,
By him imprinted, and within his power
To leave the figure or disfigure it.
Demetrius is a worthy gentleman.

Hermis: So is Lysander.

Theseus: In himself he is,
But in this kind, wanting your father's voice,
The other must be held the worthier.

Hermia: I would my father looked but with my eyes.

Theseus: Rather your eyes must with his judgement look. (Vol. 3; 1.1.41–57)

FROM *THE TWO GENTLEMEN OF VERONA*

Duke: 'Tis not unknown to thee that I have sought
To match my friend Sir Thurio to my daughter.

Valentine: I know it well, my lord; and sure the match
Were rich and honourable; besides, the gentleman
Is full of virtue, bounty, worth, and qualities
Beseeming such a wife as your fair daughter:
Cannot your Grace win her to fancy him?

Duke: No, trust me. She is peevish, sullen, froward,
Proud, disobedient, stubborn, lacking duty;
Neither regarding that she is my child,
Nor fearing me as if I were her father:
And, may I say to thee, this pride of hers,
Upon advice, hath drawn my love from her,
And, where I thought the remnant of mine age
Should have been cherish'd by her child-like duty,
I now am full resolved to take a wife,
And turn her out to who will take her in:
Then let her beauty be her wedding-dower;
For me and my possessions she esteems not. (Vol. 1; 3.1.61–79)

BIBLICAL REFERENCES TO FAMILY BONDS

Much that Shakespeare's contemporaries preached, wrote, and believed about family bonds and family responsibilities was based on the Bible. The passages below are taken from the Geneva Bible, which was the most popular and widely read English translation of the Bible in Shakespeare's day. The verses below help to show the dilemma in which Cordelia is placed at the beginning of the play. The passages from Exodus, Deuteronomy, and Ephesians, all stress that children should honor and obey their parents. Indeed this is not only commanded, but a reward for obedience to this command is also promised. Children who honor and obey their parents will have long and happy lives. But the verses from Genesis and Matthew make it clear that marriage, to some degree, cancels out previous familial commitments. The son leaves his father and becomes one flesh with his wife. So when Regan claims that she is "an enemy to all other joys" but her father's love, and that she is "alone felicitate" in her father's love, she is saying that she loves only him, and that she has no love for her husband, with whom she is supposed to have become one person (1.1.72, 74). Cordelia, according to these verses, would be right to say that she "shall never marry like [her] sisters, / To love [her] father all" (1.1.102–3).

It should also be noted that the verses from Ephesians also counsel fathers not to provoke their children to wrath, instruct servants to obey their masters as they would obey God, and advise masters to remember that they also serve a master in heaven and should rule their servants with that in mind. Most of the advice on family relationships that can be found in conduct books and sermons is based on these passages of the Bible.

FROM THE GENEVA BIBLE

Exodus 20:12

Honour thy father and thy mother, that thy days may be prolonged upon the land, which the Lord thy God giveth thee.

Deuteronomy 5:16

Honour thy father & thy mother, as the Lord thy God hath commanded thee that thy days may be prolonged, and that it may go well with thee upon the land, which the Lord thy God giveth thee.

Ephesians 6:1–9

1. Children, obey your parents in the Lord: for this is right.
2. Honour thy father and mother (which is the first commandment with promise)
3. That it may be well with thee, and that thou mayest live long on earth.
4. And ye, fathers, provoke not your children to wrath: but bring them up in instruction and information of the Lord.
5. Servants, be obedient unto them that are your masters, according to the flesh, with fear and trembling in singleness of your hearts as unto Christ,
6. Not with service to the eye, as men pleasers, but as the servants of Christ, doing the will of God from the heart,
7. With good will serving the Lord, and not men.
8. And know ye that whatsoever good thing any man doeth, that same shall he receive of the Lord, whether he be bond or free.
9. And ye masters, do the same things unto them, putting away threatening: & know that even your master also is in heaven, neither is there respect of person with him.

Genesis 2:24

Therefore shall man leave his father and his mother, and shall cleave to his wife, and they shall be one flesh.

Matthew 19: 5–6

5. . . . for this cause, shall a man leave father and mother, and cleave unto his wife, and they twain shall be one flesh.
6. Wherefore they are no more twain, but one flesh. Let not man therefore put asunder that, which God hath coupled together.

THE DUTIES OF DAUGHTERS AND WIVES

Juan Luis Vives, a Spanish humanist, wrote *The Education of a Christian Woman* (*De institutione feminae Christianae*) at the request of Queen Catherine of Aragon, the first wife of Henry VIII of England. It was written for the education of the Princess Mary, daughter of Henry VIII and Catherine of Aragon, but it reached a much wider audience, becoming a very popular book throughout the sixteenth century. The work is divided into three books discussing the intellectual and spiritual education of unmarried women, wives, and widows, respectively. Vives' work was progressive for his time in that he advocated education for women and claimed that women's intellectual abilities were equal to or greater than men's. He is, however, very traditional in other respects, and the passages below are clearly influenced by the biblical teachings on the duties of daughters and wives as well as by classical sources. Once again we see the dilemma that Cordelia faces at the beginning of *King Lear*. As a daughter she is to love and obey her father, but as a young woman on the brink of marriage, she should be preparing to become one person with a husband who, according to Vives, will substitute for all other family relations. Vives expands on the verses from Genesis and Matthew, cited above, suggesting that the daughter, as well as the son, must leave her parents and join in marriage with her husband.

FROM JUAN LUIS VIVES, *THE INSTRUCTION OF A CHRISTIAN WOMAN*, TRANS. RICHARD HYRDE (1529)

(London, 1529; STC 24856)

From Book One, Chapter Fifteen, How a Maiden Ought to Love

And yet I would not a maid should clearly be without love, for mankinde seemeth to be made and shapen unto love.... Wherefore the maid shall have to love the father almighty god, her spouse Christ, and his mother the holy virgin, and the church of God with all the holy virgins whose souls dwell blessedly in heaven.... She hath also her own father and mother, which brought her into the world and brought her up and nourished with so great labour and care, whom she ought to have in the stead [place] of god and love and worship and help with all her power. Therefore let her regard greatly their commandments and meekly obey them. Neither show in mind, countenance or gesture any stubbornness, but reckon them to be as it were the very image of almighty god, the father of all things. (B iii v-r)

From Book Two, Chapter Four, How She Shall Behave Unto Her Husband

It were a long matter and hard to express and thereto wondrous if I should rehearse every point of the wife's duty unto her husband. Our lord comprehendeth it in the gospel with one word. Therefore let us remember how we have said before that she is as one body with her husband. Wherefore she ought to love him none otherwise than her self. I have said before, and oft shall again, for this is the greatest virtue of a married woman. This is the thing that wedlock signifieth and commandeth, that the wife should reckon to have her husband for both father, mother, brethren and sisters, like as Adam was unto Eve, and as the most noble and chaste woman Andromache said her husband Hector was unto her in these words:

> Thou art unto me both father and mother,
> My own dear husband and well beloved brother.

And if it be true that men do say that friendship maketh one heart of two, much more truly and effectually ought wedlock to do the same, which far passeth [in] all manner both friendship and kindred. Therefore it is not said that wedlock doth make one man or one mind or one body of two, but clearly one person. Wherefore the words that the man spake of the woman, saying for her sake a man should leave both father and mother and bide with his wife, the same words the woman ought both to say and think with more reason. For although there be one made of two, yet the woman is as daughter unto her husband, and of nature more weaker. Wherefore she needeth his aid and succour. Wherefore if she be destitute of her husband, deserted and left alone, she may soon take hurt and wrong. Therefore if she be with her husband, where he is, there hath she both her country, her house, her father, her mother, her friends, and all her treasure. (Xiii r–Xiii 2 v)

THE DUTIES OF CHILDREN TO THEIR PARENTS

In Bartholomew Batty's sixteenth-century conduct book, *A Christian Man's Closet,* he elaborates on the duties that children owe to their parents. He not only instructs children to love, honor, and obey their parents, but he claims that this should be done even when the parents are old, senile, or foolish. Furthermore, when the parents become old, the children are to care for them, and provide for them, while still treating them with respect and honor. Neither the "infirmity of [Lear's] age," nor the fact that he has "ever but slenderly known himself" (1.1.291–2) would, in Batty's opinion, excuse his children for not showing him respect and love or for not deferring to his judgment and authority. And certainly Batty would feel that the children of Lear and Gloucester had a duty to care for their elderly fathers, even carrying them on their backs if necessary. Children, according to Batty, are even responsible for causing "their parents to be loving and good unto them" by "showing themselves obedient and good children." Batty would hold the children of Lear and Gloucester responsible for any unloving behavior demonstrated by these fathers.

Cordelia (Ann Calder-Marshall) forgives and tends to her ailing father (Laurence Olivier) in director Michael Elliot's 1984 televised version of Shakespeare's *King Lear*. Reprinted with permission of Photofest.

FROM BARTHOLOMEW BATTY, *A CHRISTIAN MAN'S CLOSET,* TRANS. WILLIAM LOWTH (1581)

(London, 1581; STC 2nd ed. 1591)

To honor Parents, is to deem and judge honorably of them, for that God hath made us subject unto them, for by the determinate will and appointment of God, they are to govern, and we to obey. And therefore with all our hearts, we must submit ourselves unto their wisdom, justice, judgment and authority. And albeit they shall sometime offend and err in performing their duties (as it is the nature of all men) yet must we pardon, excuse, and cover their faults most lovingly and reverently. For whereas Saint Paul saith: Honor thy father and mother...he requireth this one thing of children, that with all their hearts, they love, reverence, & aid their parents to the uttermost of their power, and also those to whom their Parents have committed them, that is to say, Magistrates, Elders, Preachers, Masters, Teachers, Tutors and such like. Therefore to honor Parents is not only to salute them humbly, to speak to them lovingly, and to use them courteously, to put off the cap before them, to give them the way and upper hand in every place: But also the holy Scriptures do teach children to obey their parents, to serve them, to fear, love, honor, and reverence them, not only in words and outward show, but in their hearts and minds also: To follow their godly precepts and examples of life: and patiently to take correction at their hands: To make continual and hearty prayers unto God for them, and to relieve and nourish their Parents in case they fall into poverty and decay. And when they are old, to guide, lead, yea & bear them on their shoulders if need require and in all pointes by showing themselves obedient and good children, to move their Parents to be loving and good unto them.....

True Honour consisteth in this, that we think and judge worthily of our parents, that we regard them most honorably, that we yield and give all reverence unto their authority and judgment: that we never condemn or despise them, be they never so poor, old, and crooked, yea, if they did seem to dote, and were very wayward, to prefer the title and name of father and mother, before all faults whatsoever. Neither to regard or esteem what manner of parents, but to rejoice & be glad that we have parents. For although thou shalt be promoted to great worship and honor, yet oughtest thou to be thankful to thy poor and base father, to whom next unto God thou art most bound for the same. (63r-62v [pages are numbered out- of-order])

You say very truly, for Parents are to be honored after three sorts chiefly, First children shall truly love their parents with all their hearts and mind. They shall give unto them all high dignity and reverence. They shall so esteem of them, as that no treasure in the world ought to be more dear and precious unto them. Secondly they shall honour them with words and good manners, showing unto them all kind of reverence that may be, they may not curse them, nor chat or mutter against them, but rather suffer them patiently, albeit they be more wayward, hard, & eager, than either reason or wisdom doth require. Thirdly, they must also honor them with their labor, pains & travel (that is to say) they shall help, relieve and provide for them, both with their bodies & goods: and in no wise suffer them to be oppressed with poverty and misery when they grow aged. And children shall do this, not only willingly, but also reverently, and with great lowliness of mind, as though this duty and benefit, should be done to God him self (as it is in very deed) & they ought to be right thankful unto God which hath thus preferred them to this worship and honour, and hath made them thus able to perform this duty. (65v)

THE DUTY OF RECOMPENSE

William Gouge, a puritan preacher, also details the duties of children in his *Of Domesticall Duties*. In the first passage below he specifically discusses the duty of "recompense," or the duty of children to repay their parents for the trouble and care of having raised them. This is, essentially, what Cordelia speaks of when she answers Lear's love test:

> Good my lord,
> You have begot me, bred me, loved me; I
> Return those duties back as are right fit,
> Obey you, love you, and most honor you. (1.1.94–7)

Lear, however, fails to recognize this as the virtue of recompense, and instead hears only that Cordelia's words are less flattering than those of Goneril and Regan.

The second and third passages below elaborate on the duty or recompense and what it entails. According to Gouge, children, having been cared for when they were weak and helpless, should care for their weak or aged parents, continuing to respect them while providing them with what they need. Regan and Goneril clearly fail to recompense their father when they scoff at his "poor judgement" and "the infirmity of his age" (1.1.289, 291).

FROM WILLIAM GOUGE, *OF DOMESTICALL DUTIES: EIGHT TREATISES* (1622), TREATISE 5, *DUTIES OF CHILDREN*

(London, 1622)

From Chapter 39, Of Children's Recompense

The general head whereunto all the duties which children owe to their parents in regard of their *Necessity*, is in one word *Recompense*, which is a duty whereby children endeavor as much as in them lieth, to repay what they can for their parent's kindness, care, and cost towards them, and that in way of thankfulness; which maketh a childe think he cannot do too much for his parent, & well may he think so, for a parent doth much more for his childe before it is able to do for itself, than the childe possibly can do for the parent. So as if the parent's *authority* were laid aside, yet the law of *equity* requireth this duty of *Recompense:* so also doth the law of *piety* and *charity*. Wherefore of all other Duties this is most due. It is in express terms given in charge to children by the Apostle, who willeth them to learn to *requite their parents*.

Contrary is neglect of parents in their need, which is more than monstrous ingratitude. As all ingratitude is odious to God and man, so this most of all, and yet very many are guilty thereof. In them the proverb is verified that *love is weighty.* For it is the property of weighty things to fall down apace but to ascend slowly, and that not without some violence. Thus love from the parent to the childe falleth down apace, but it hardly ascendeth from children to parents. In which respect another proverb saith, *One father will better nourish nine children, than nine children one father.* Many children in this kind do no more for their parents, than for strangers. They either consider not how much their parents have done for them; or else they conceit [think] that what their parents did, was of mere duty, and needeth no recompense. Fie upon such barbarous and inhumane children! (469–70)

From Chapter 41, Of Children's Bearing with Their Parents' Infirmities

Children bear with their parents' infirmities when they do not the less reverently esteem their place, or person, nor perform the less duty to them because of their infirmities.

This is the first particular branch of recompense. For children in their younger and weaker years are subject to many infirmities: if parents had the less respected them for their infirmities, and from thence had taken occasion to neglect them, and would not have borne with them, surely they could not have been so well brought up. That great patience, long-sufferance, and much forbearance which parents have showed towards their children, requireth that children in way of recompense show the like to their parents as occasion is offered....

Contrary to this duty do they, who take occasion from their parents' infirmities to think basely of their person and their place, and thereupon grow careless in duty, either refusing to do any duty at all, or else doing it carelessly, grudgingly, disdainfully, and scornfully.... The law that threateneth God's vengeance against such children as *mock at their father, or despise to obey their mother,* maketh no exception of parents' infirmities. (470–71)

From Chapter 44, Of Children's Relieving Their Parents According to Their Need

Besides bearing with parents' necessities, in such cases as parents stand in need of their children's relief and succor, they must afford it them. In sickness they must visit them, as *Joseph* visited his father. In time of mourning, they must comfort them, as the children of *Jaakob.* In want, they must provide things needful for them, as the sons of *Jaakob,* who went up to buy food for their father, and as *Joseph,* who sent for *Jaakob* into Egypt, and there nourished him. It is noted of *Ruth,* that she did not only glean for her mother a poor woman, but also reserved some of that food which was given to her self to eat, for her. In time of danger they must do what they can for their protection and preservation.... (473)

PARENTS' RESPONSIBILITIES

William Gouge also outlines the responsibilities that parents owe to their children. In the first and third passages below, Gouge notes that parents are to provide for their children in all ways and at all times, and that they are also to provide their children with a suitable spouse. In the second passage, Gouge criticizes the foolishness of parents who give too much control to their children and give up their own authority. Lear, of course, is a prime example of this folly, as he gives up the authority and power of kingship while expecting to retain the privileges and pleasures of the office. He has also failed in his duties as a father by disowning Cordelia and depriving her of the dowry that would, even without the generosity and insight of the King of France, allow her to find a suitable husband.

FROM WILLIAM GOUGE, *OF DOMESTICALL DUTIES: EIGHT TREATISES* (1622), TREATISE 6, *DUTIES OF PARENTS*

(London, 1622)

From Chapter 8, Of Parents' Providence for Their Children

The *head,* whereunto all the particular duties, which parents owe to their children, may be referred, is *a provident care for their children's good.* This extendeth itself to *all times,* and to *all things.*

To *all times,* as to the infancy, youth, and man-age of their children; and that not only while parents live, but after their departure.

To *all things,* namely, tending both to the *temporal good* of their children, and also to their *spiritual good.*

Children are the very substance of their parents, & therefore ought parents so far to seek their children's good as their own. (505)

From Chapter 41, Of Parents' Folly in Letting Go All Their Power over Their Children

Contrary is their folly who put themselves in their children's power, and let go all their authority over them. Many parents that have thus done, having by woeful experience found the mischief and inconvenience that hath followed thereupon, have much repented their folly, and used means of redress, but all too late. For a mischief is much more easily prevented than redressed. All the power that *David* had could not hold in *Absolom* after he was permitted to have horses, and chariots, and men at his command. If *David,* as he begun, had continued to keep him within a compass, and still held him under, all the treasonable plots which he put in execution, might easily have been prevented. Our times afford too many examples of parents' folly in this kind, and of the mischiefes following thereupon. (548)

From Chapter 53, Of Parents' Care in Providing Fit Marriages for Their Children

God hath further laid a charge upon parents to provide marriages for their children: for thus saith the Prophet in the name of the Lord unto parents, *Take wives to your sons and give your daughters to husbands:* [Jer. 29:6] and thus the Apostle, *If any man think that he behaveth himself uncomely toward his virgin, if she pass the flower of her age, and need so require, let them marry* [1 Cor. 7:36]. This direction was given in times of persecution, when by reason of the present necessity it was better not to marry: if then a parent ought to be careful (*need requiring*) to provide a marriage for his daughter, much more ought he in times of peace. Holy parents commended by the Holy Ghost have been careful in performing this duty, as *Abraham, Isaak, Naomi,* and others: yea *Hagar* had learned this duty in *Abraham's* house. But the perfect pattern (which surpasseth all other examples) is of God himself, who provided a fit match for his *son Adam.* (563)

ILLEGITIMACY AND INHERITANCE

In the late-sixteenth century a lawyer, Henry Swinburne, wrote an important legal treatise on wills and inheritance. The following excerpt from Swinburne's *Treatise of Testaments,* shows the complexity of the legal situation regarding illegitimacy and inheritance. The civil courts and the ecclesiastical courts did not always agree on the matter, and there were loopholes in both sets of laws. Thus, while it would have been customary for Gloucester to leave his entire estate to his eldest and legitimate son, Edgar, and to leave his younger, illegitimate son, Edmund, either nothing, or merely enough to maintain himself, it would have been possible for him to disinherit Edgar and leave everything to Edmund. This is clearly Edmund's plan, and it is the reason that he forges a letter from his brother and uses it to convince Gloucester of Edgar's treachery. This is the "danger whereunto lawfull children are subject" which Swinburne discusses at the end of this excerpt. While Swinburne praises the ecclesiastical courts for allowing supposed fathers to provide for their illegitimate children rather than leaving them either to be a burden on the parish or to suffer for the sins of their parents, he condemns the leniency of this other loophole or "limitation" of the law which would otherwise prevent bastards from inheriting. He claims that the mothers of the illegitimate children may convince men to disinherit their lawful and deserving children. Edmund, of course, does the convincing himself and does not need the help of his mother, of whom nothing is said except that she was attractive.

FROM HENRY SWINBURNE, *TREATISE OF TESTAMENTS,* PART 5

(London, 1635)

Bastards begotten and borne in *Adultery* or *Incest,* are not capable of any benefit by the Testament or last Will of their incestuous or adulterous parents, which conclusion is accompanied with no small train of ampliations and limitations, of which company these are not the meanest.... (13)

Thirdly, by the Laws Ecclesiastical they are also capable of so much of that which is bequeathed unto them by their incestuous and adulterous parents, as will suffice for their competent alimentation or relief: that is to say, for their food, clothing, lodging, and other meet and convenient necessaries, according to the wealthy and ability of the parents, and although the civil Law in detestation of this heinous sin of incest and adultery did deprive this incestuous and adulterous issue of the hope of all testamentary benefit, though it were left for, and in the name of alimentation or needful relief, the rather by this mean to restrain the unbridled lusts of some, and to preserve the chastity of others: nevertheless, forasmuch as Nature hath taught all creatures to provide for their young, so that the very brute beasts have a natural care to bring up whatsoever they bring forth. Seeing also in equity the poor infants ought not to be punished (at least not to perish for want of food, by occasion of the father's fault, whereof they are altogether faultless): Therefore the Ecclesiastical Law, whereby not only adulterous, but incestuous issue also is made capable of so much as is sufficient for needful and convenient sustentation, hath prevailed against the rigor of the Civil Law, and is to be observed especially in the Ecclesiastical Court, as more agreeable to Nature, Equity, and Humanity.

Wherefore if the Testator shall bequeath a competent portion to his base daughter, for her preferment in marriage, the same is due and recoverable in the Ecclesiastical Court: but if the sum bequeathed be excessive, then is it to be moderated... and to be reduced into a convenient portion.

And in this respect the Laws and Statutes of this Realm, in providing as well for the Convenient relief and keeping of poor and miserable children, begotten and borne out of lawful matrimony, at the charges of the reputed father and mother, (without distinction whether such infants were begotten in Incest and Adultery, or Fornication) as for the punishment of the mother, and reputed father of such unlawful issue, are worthily commended, although in respect of the next limitation following, they may seem not altogether so worthy commendation.

The fourth limitation is grounded in the Laws of this Realm, which do permit every man, both by deed made and executed during their lives, and also by their last Wills and Testaments to be executed after their deaths, to give and to devise unto any their Bastards without distinction, all their Lands, Tenements, or Hereditaments, without restraint, at the least more than will suffice for their sustentation and much more than they are worthy of. Which thing cannot but redound to the great prejudice of right heirs, considering the danger whereunto lawful children are subject, and which they do many times sustain through the forcible flatteries of vile dissembling Harlots, no less void of all modesty, than full fraught with all kind of subtlety, with whose sweet poison and pleasant sting many men are so charmed and enchanted, that they have neither power to hearken to the just petitions of a virtuous wife, praying and craving for her children, nor grace to deny the unjust demands of a vicious and a shameless whore, prating and grating for her bastards.... (15–17)

SERVANTS AND MASTERS

Conduct manuals and sermons did not limit themselves to talking about the duties and responsibilities of parents and children. Servants were also considered to be part of the household or family unit, and the duties of servants and the responsibilities of masters to their servants were often outlined in such texts. In Henry Smith's sermon, *A Preparative to Marriage,* he discusses the role of servants in the household, placing them a small step below children. They are not children, but they are under the care and supervision of the master, and he should treat them with a "fatherly care" and remember that he himself is a servant to God. This may help to illuminate the paternal feelings that Lear seems to have for the Fool. Even when he is going mad and wandering on the heath, Lear can feel pity and concern for his fool who has followed him into this misery. William Gouge also discusses the duties of masters and servants, and he asserts that servants are always to obey their masters, unless the master asks them to do something that goes against the commands of God. If a master asks them to commit a sin, they are to obey God rather than their master. Gouge would most likely have approved of the behavior of Kent and the nameless servant of Cornwall. Both men were willing to go against the commands of their masters because they felt their masters were asking them to commit a sin. Kent refuses to lie to Lear even though Lear wants to hear lies. Cornwall's servant tries to prevent Cornwall from gouging out the eyes of Gloucester. Not only do both men feel that they are doing what is right, they also argue that they are serving their masters more faithfully by disobeying their unjust commands and trying to prevent their unjust behavior. Cornwall's servant tells Cornwall that though he has served him since he was a child, he has never done him "better service" than he does him now by opposing him (3.7.75).

FROM HENRY SMITH, *A PREPARATIVE TO MARRIAGE AND TWO OTHER SERMONS*

(London, 1591)

It is not a base nor a vile thing to be called a servant, for our Lord is called a servant, which teacheth Christians to use their servants well for Christ's sake, seeing they are servants too, and have one master Christ. As *David* speaketh of man, saying, *Thou hast made him a little lower than the Angels* [Ps 8:6]: So I may say of servants, that God hath made them a little lower than children, not children, but the next to children, as one would say inferiour children, or sons in law: and therefore the householder is called *Paterfamilias,* which signifieth a father of his family, because he should have a fatherly care over his servants, as if they were his children, and not use them only for their labor like beasts. Beside, the name of a servant does not signify suffering, but doing: therefore masters must not exercise their hands upon them, but set their hands to work: and yet as God laieth no more upon his servants than he makes them able to bear; so men should lay no more upon their servants than they are able to bear. For a good man (saith *Salomon*) is merciful to his beast, and therefore he will be more merciful to his brother [Provs 12:10]. That man is not worthy to be served which cannot afford that his servants should serve God as well as himself. Give unto God that which is God's and then thou maiest take that which is thine. (93–4)

FROM WILLIAM GOUGE, *OF DOMESTICALL DUTIES: EIGHT TREATISES* (1622), TREATISE 7, *DUTIES OF SERVANTS*

(London, 1622)

From Chapter 38, Of Servants Forbearing to Obey Their Master against God"

That the extent of servant's obedience be not too far stretched, the Apostle setteth down an excellent limitation thereof: and that in these four phrases, *As unto Christ, As the servants of Christ, Doing the will of God, As to the Lord;* all which do show that the *obedience which servants yield to their master must be such as may stand with their obedience to Christ.* So that if masters command their servants never so peremptorily to do any unlawful thing, that is any thing forbidden by God's word, they may not yield to it.... Thus if a master should command his servant to kill, to steal, to forswear himself, to lie, to use false measures and weights, to go to masse, or doe any other unlawful thing, he ought not to obey him.

Again, if masters forbid their servants to do that which God hath commanded them to do, they must, notwithstanding their master's prohibition, do it.... So if a profane or popish master shall forbid his servant to go to Church, or to hear the word, or to take the Sacrament, or to dwell with his wife if he be married, or to make restitution of that which he hath fraudulently gotten, or any other bounden duty, herein they must say, *we ought to obey God rather than men.* For when masters command and forbid any thing against God, they go beyond their commission, and therein their authority ceaseth. (637–8)

QUESTIONS FOR WRITTEN AND ORAL DISCUSSION

1. Consider the families of Lear and Gloucester and the documents about family life provided in this chapter. With these in mind, what similarities do you see between

families in Shakespeare's day and families now? What emotions and responsibilities do we share in common with the families of 400 years ago? What has changed?

2. Lear brings much of his tragedy on himself, but his two eldest daughters also betray him, and some critics have argued that Cordelia is also partially responsible for the tragedy that befalls her father and her kingdom since she knew her father wanted to be flattered and yet she answered his love test with very unflattering, almost legalistic language, giving him precisely half her love, and stating that she loves him only according to her bond, "No more, nor less" (1.1.91–2). Divide into four groups and have each group determine the level of responsibility that each member of Lear's family (Lear, Goneril, Regan, and Cordelia) bears for the tragedy. What did each do wrong, or, if you feel a family member is not responsible, what makes you feel that way?

3. Read Edmund's speech at 1.2.1–22 and the excerpt from Swinburne's *Treatise of Testaments*. In light of the treatment of illegitimate children in Shakespeare's time, do you feel any sympathy for Edmund? Why or why not?

4. Read the excerpts provided from other Shakespeare plays dealing with fathers and daughters. What similarities do you see between these relationships and the relationship between Lear and Cordelia? What is different?

5. Read act one, scene one, carefully in light of what Vives and Gouge say about the duties of children and daughters. Do you think Cordelia was right to refuse to swear all of her love to her father, or should she have obeyed him since he was still her father and she was not yet married?

6. Read what Batty says about the duties of children to their parents. Does Cordelia love and honor her father in the way that Batty instructs? Do Regan and Goneril? Where, if anywhere, does each one fall short of these instructions?

7. Both Batty and Gouge assert that children should care for their aged or infirm parents, providing them with anything they might need. Does Edgar care for Gloucester as he should, or should he have comforted his father by revealing his identity earlier?

8. In act 3, scene 4, Lear puts Regan and Goneril through an imaginary trial. What are the charges? Are they guilty? Stage the trial, with students acting as the prosecutor, defense, and jury, and determine whether or not they are guilty and of what crimes.

9. In Shakespeare's day servants were considered part of the household, and almost part of the family. They were expected to serve their masters loyally, only disobeying them if their command required them to commit a sin. In light of this, is Kent right to oppose Lear in act one, scene one? Is Cornwall's servant in act three, scene seven, right to oppose his master? Is the Fool right to criticize Lear?

10. What is your opinion of the custom of primogeniture? Is it better to divide an estate between several children, as Lear does, or to give almost everything to one child and so keep the estate or kingdom intact?

11. Assemble the characters of *Lear* for a session of family counseling. One student should play the part of a counselor while others play the parts of the various charac-

ters. Each student should study his or her character carefully and be prepared to act in-character. The counselor can then advise them either according to the dictates of Renaissance conduct books or according to more modern ideas of family behavior. After conducting the therapy session write up an explanation of how family dynamics might have been improved from your character's point of view.

12. Which family members follow the dictates of the conduct books and sermons of Shakespeare's day and which do not? What does this suggest about Shakespeare's view of these rules for family behavior? Is he criticizing these rules or emphasizing the need for them?

13. Choose one character from *King Lear* and write a one- to two-page explanation, from that character's point of view, of what is wrong with that character's family. Does Regan blame everything on her father's senility? What would Cordelia say is the problem? What might Edmund or Edgar say about their family?

14. Cordelia, like many Shakespearian heroines, is forced to choose between obedience to her father and love of a future husband. Do you think a person should feel more bound to his/her parents or to a spouse?

15. Compare Lear and Gloucester as fathers. Do they make the same mistakes? Does one make more mistakes than the other? In what ways are they good fathers?

16. Many critics have noted that there are no mothers in *King Lear*. Presumably the mothers of Lear's daughters and Gloucester's sons died before the beginning of the play. In your opinion, and based on your experiences, how might the family dynamics have been changed by the presence of mothers? Would things have gone better if there had been mothers present, or would the tragedy still have occurred?

17. One of the duties of children, according to Gouge, is to bear with their parents' weaknesses and to help disguise these weaknesses as much as possible. Regan, Goneril, and Edmund all exploit the weaknesses of their parents. Do Cordelia and Edgar bear with and disguise the weaknesses of their parents? Do they in any way exploit the weaknesses of their parents?

18. Read the excerpt from Swinburne's *Treatise of Testaments*. What is your opinion of the laws regarding illegitimacy and inheritance? Do you agree with Swinburne that allowing illegitimate children to inherit endangers legitimate children?

19. Do the masters in *King Lear* take "fatherly care" of their servants as Smith says they should? Which do and which do not? Give specific examples from the play.

SUGGESTED READING

Boose, Lynda E. "The Father and the Bride." *Shakespeare's Middle Tragedies: A Collection of Critical Essays*. Ed. David Young. Englewood Cliffs, NJ: Prentice Hall, 1993.

Dreher, Diane Elizabeth. *Domination and Defiance: Fathers and Daughters in Shakespeare*. Lexington: UP of Kentucky, 1986.

Findlay, Allison. *Illegitimate Power: Bastards in Renaissance Drama.* Manchester, GB: Manchester UP, 1994.

Klein, Joan Larsen, ed. *Daughters, Wives and Widows: Writings by Men about Women and Marriage in England: 1500–1640.* Urbana: U of Illinois P, 1992.

Laslett, Peter, Karla Oosterveen, and Richard M. Smith, eds. *Bastardy and its Comparative History.* Cambridge, MA: Harvard UP, 1980.

5

Adaptations: A Tale Retold

Since Shakespeare's *King Lear* is itself an adaptation and a retelling of earlier stories, as discussed in chapter one, it is not surprising that the play has been retold and adapted since Shakespeare's time. Adaptations do not simply repeat a story, but retell it with some important change. They might, for instance, change the setting of the play or the perspective from which it is told. These changes can alter the focus of the story, highlighting an issue that was only touched on in the original, or exploring a central theme from a different point of view. Shakespeare's play is still performed, but the play has also been adapted in various ways. This chapter will explore three of the many adaptations of Shakespeare's *King Lear,* ranging from a late-seventeenth-century play to a twentieth-century novel and two films. Each adaptation highlights a different issue in the play, and exploring these adaptations may help readers to better understand the issues in the original play.

NAHUM TATE'S *KING LEAR*

In 1681, about 75 years after the first performance of Shakespeare's play, a playwright named Nahum Tate revived the play, but rewrote it to suit the popular tastes of his time. His changes were substantial. He made the language easier to understand, eliminated the Fool, added a friend and confidante for Cordelia, incorporated a love story involving Edgar and Cordelia, made Edmund an even worse villain who tries to assault Cordelia, and added a happy ending in which Lear regains his kingdom and then bestows it on Cordelia and Edgar before retiring to a quiet location to spend his remaining years exchanging stories with Kent and Gloucester.

In Tate's dedicatory letter to Thomas Boteler, he explains the reasons for many of his alterations. Tate and Boteler both view Shakespeare's play as "a heap of jewels, unstrung and unpolished." That is, they see it as valuable and full of potential, but in need of organization and refinement. Tate is attempting to preserve the value while polishing the rough edges. The love story of Cordelia and Edgar, he argues, gives the story "regularity and probability"— it strings together the jewels. Lear, at the opening of Tate's adaptation, is preparing to marry off all three of his daughters, and is dividing his kingdom into their three dowers. Her love for Edgar gives Cordelia an additional motive for resisting Lear's love test at the beginning of the play, since she would prefer to be left dowerless rather than to be forced to marry Burgundy with a third of the kingdom for her dower. Her cold speech to her father is an intentional attempt to anger him so that he will disinherit her. Edgar's love for Cordelia also makes his disguise not simply "a poor shift to save his life" but a means of staying near Cordelia, who has rejected him. She is, in fact, performing her own version of Lear's love test. She has learned that Burgundy was only interested in her when she was likely to inherit a third of the kingdom, and she wants to test Edgar's love. If he will continue to love her when she has no kingdom and no dowry, then she will know that his love is true.

Tate also notes that he ends the play happily, rather than "[encumbering] the stage with dead bodies," and though he says that he worried about making so great a change, he was relieved when he saw that his audience liked it. Although most modern readers and critics prefer Shakespeare's play and seldom read Tate's version, many people in the seventeenth and eighteenth centuries, including the literary critic, Samuel Johnson, preferred Tate's version of *King Lear*. As you read Tate's dedicatory letter and the excerpt from the final scene, ask yourself what you think of the revisions he made. Spelling and punctuations have been modernized where necessary for the sake of clarity.

FROM NAHUM TATE, LETTER TO THOMAS BOTELER, IN NAHUM TATE, *THE HISTORY OF KING LEAR* (1681)

(London, 1681)

To My Esteemed Friend, Thomas Boteler, Esq;

Sir, You have a natural right to the piece, since, by your advice, I attempted the revival of it with alterations. Nothing but the power of your persuasion, and my zeal for all the remains of Shakespeare, could have wrought me to so bold an undertaking. I found that the new-modeling of this story, would force me sometimes on the difficult task of making the chiefest persons speak something like their character, on matter whereof I had no ground in my author. Lear's real, and Edgar's pretended madness have so much of extravagant nature (I know not how else to express it) as could never have started but from our Shakespeare's creating fancy. The images and language are so odd and surprising, and yet so agreeable and proper, that whilst we grant that none but Shakespeare could have formed such conceptions, yet we are satisfied that they were the only things in the world that ought to be said on those occasions. I found the whole to answer your account of it, a heap of jewels, unstrung and unpolished; yet so dazzling in their disorder, that I soon perceived I had seized a treasure. 'Twas my good Fortune to light on one expedient to rectify what was wanting in the regularity and probability of the tale, which was to run though the whole a love betwixt Edgar and Cordelia, that never changed word with each other in the original. This renders Cordelia's indifference and her father's passion in the first scene probable. It likewise gives countenance to Edgar's disguise, making that a generous design that was before a poor shift to save his life. The distress of the story is evidently heightened by it; and it particularly gave occasion of a new scene or two, of more success (perhaps) that merit. This method necessarily threw me on making the tale conclude in a success to the innocent distressed persons: Otherwise I must have encumbered the stage with dead bodies, which conduct makes many tragedies conclude with unseasonable jests. Yet was I racked with no small fears for so bold a change, till I found it well received by my audience. . . .

. . . . Many faults I see in the following pages, and question not but you will discover more; yet I will presume so far on your friendship, as to make the whole a present to you, and subscribe myself.

Your obliged friend and humble servant,
N. Tate
(A2r–A3v)

FROM NAHUM TATE, THE FINAL SCENE, IN NAHUM TATE, *THE HISTORY OF KING LEAR* (1681)

   The final scene of Tate's *King Lear* follows. As you read it, pay attention to the differences between this scene and the final scene of Shakespeare's *King Lear*. Notice, for instance, that in Shakespeare's play, characters talk of unbearable sorrows, of hearts bursting with grief, and of the inability to bear any additional suffering. In Tate's play, of course, this bursting imagery is altered. Instead of bursting with grief, Tate's characters are bursting with joy. Also, Lear, who in Shakespeare's play laments his inability to save Cordelia's life, though he did kill the man who was hanging her, is able, in Tate's play, to rescue Cordelia by killing two of the would-be assassins. What other changes do you notice?

Act 5, scene 3

Scene, A prison.
Lear asleep, with his head on Cordelia's Lap.

Cordelia: What toils, thou wretched King, hast thou endured
To make thee draw, in chains, a sleep so sound?
Thy better angel charm thy ravished mind
With fancied freedom, peace is used to lodge
On cottage straw, Thou hast the beggar's bed,
Therefore shouldst have the beggar's careless thought.
And now, my Edgar, I remember thee,
What fate has seized thee in this general wreck
I know not, but I know thou must be wretched
Because Cordelia holds thee dear.
O Gods! A sudden gloom overwhelms me, and the image
Of death overspreads the place. Ha! Who are these?

Enter Captain and Officers with cords.

Captain: Now, Sirs, dispatch, already you are paid
In part, the best of your reward's to come.

Lear: Charge, charge upon their flank, their last wing halts;
Push, push the battle, and the day's our own.
Their ranks are broke, down, down with Albany.
Who holds my hands?—Oh thou deceiving Sleep,
I was this very minute on the chase;
And now a prisoner here—what mean the slaves?
You will not murder me?

Cordelia: Help Earth and Heaven!
For your souls' sakes, dear Sirs, and for the Gods.

Officer: No tears, good lady, no pleading against gold and preferment;
Come sirs, make ready your cords.

Cordelia: You, sir, I'll seize,
You have a humane form, and if no prayers
Can touch your soul to spare a poor King's life,
If there be any thing that you hold dear,
By that I beg you to dispatch me first.

Captain: Comply with her request, dispatch her first

Lear: Off Hell-hounds, by the Gods I charge you spare her
'Tis my Cordelia, my true pious daughter.
No Pity?—Nay, then take an old Man's Vengeance.

Snatches a Partizan, and strikes down two of them; the rest quit Cordelia, and turn upon him. Enter Edgar and Albany.

Edgar: Death! Hell! Ye vultures hold your impious hands,
Or take a speedier death than you would give.

Captain: By whose command?

Edgar: Behold the Duke your Lord.

Albany: Guards, seize those instruments of cruelty.

Cordelia: My Edgar, Oh!

Edgar: My dear Cordelia, Lucky was the minute
Of our approach, the Gods have weighed our sufferings
We are past the fire, and now must shine to ages.

Gentleman: Look here, my Lord, see where the generous King
Has slain two of them.

Lear: Did I not, fellow?
I've seen the day, with my good biting Falchion
I could have made 'em skip. I am old now,
And these vile crosses spoil me. Out of breath!
Fie, oh! Quite out of breath and spent.

Albany: Bring in old Kent, and, Edgar, guide you hither
Your father, whom you said was near,
He may be an Ear-witness at the least
Of our proceedings.

Exit Edgar. Kent brought in here.

Lear: Who are you?
My eyes are none of the best, I'll tell you straight.
Oh Albany! Well, sir, we are your captives,
And you are come to see death pass upon us.

Why this delay?—or is it your Highness's pleasure
To give us first the torture? Say ye so?
Why here's old Kent and I, as tough a pair
As ever bore Tyrant's stroke:—but my Cordelia,
My poor Cordelia here, O Pity!

Albany: Take off their chains—Thou injured Majesty,
The wheel of fortune now has made her circle,
And blessing yet stand 'twixt thy grave and thee.

Lear: Com'st thou, inhumane Lord, to sooth us back
To a fool's paradise of hope, to make
Our doom more wretched? Go too, we are too well
Acquainted with misfortune to be gulled
With lying hope. No we will hope no more.

Albany: I have a tale to unfold so full of wonder
As cannot meet an easy Faith;
But by that royal injured head 'tis true.

Kent: What would your highness?

Albany: Know the noble Edgar
Impeached Lord Edmund since the fight, of treason,
And dared him for the proof to single combat,
In which the Gods confirmed his charge by conquest.
I left even now the traitor wounded mortally.

Lear: And whither tends this story?

Albany: E'er they fought
Lord Edgar gave into my hands this paper,
A blacker scroll of treason, and of lust
Than can be found in the records of Hell.
There, sacred sir, behold the character
Of Gonerill the worst of daughters, but
More vicious wife.

Cordelia: Could there be yet addition to their guilt?
What will not they that wrong a father do?

Albany: Since then my injuries, Lear, fall in with thine:
I have resolved to same redress for both.

Kent: What says my Lord?

Cordelia: Speak, for me thought I heard
The charming voice of a descending God.

Albany: The troops by Edmund raised, I have disbanded.
Those that remain are under my command.
What comfort may be brought to cheer your age
And heal your savage wrongs, shall be applied.

For to your majesty we do resign
Your kingdom, save what part your self conferred
On us in marriage.

Kent: Hear you that, my liege?

Cordelia: Then there are Gods, and virtue is their care.

Lear: Is it possible?
Let the spheres stop their course, the sun make halt
The winds be hushed, the seas and fountains rest.
All nature pause and listen to the change.
Where is my Kent, my Caius.

Kent: Here, my liege.

Lear: Why I have news that will recall thy youth
Ha! Didst thou hear it, or did the inspiring Gods
Whisper to me alone? Old Lear shall be
A King again.

Kent: The Prince, that like a God has Power, has said it.

Lear: Cordelia then shall be a Queen, mark that:
Cordelia shall be Queen. Winds catch the sound
And bear it on your rosie wings to Heaven.
Cordelia is a Queen.

Albany: Look, sir, where pious Edgar comes
Leading his eye-less father. O my liege!
His wondrous story will deserve your leisure,
What he has done and suffered for your sake,
What for the fair Cordelia's.

Gloster: Where is my liege? Conduct me to his knees to hail
His second birth of Empire. My dear Edgar
Has, with himself, revealed the King's blessed restoration.

Lear: My poor dark Gloster.

Gloster: O let me kiss that once more sceptered hand!

Lear: Hold, thou mistakest the Majesty. Kneel here,
Cordelia has our power. Cordelia's queen.
Speak, is not that noble suffering Edgar?

Gloster: My pious son, more dear than my lost eyes.

Lear: I wronged him too, but here's the fair amends.

Edgar: Your leave, my liege, for an unwelcome message.
Edmund (but that's a trifle) is expired.
What more will touch you, your imperious daughters,
Gonerill and haughty Regan, both are dead,
Each by the other poisoned at a banquet.
This, dying, they confessed.

Cordelia: O fatal period of ill-governed life!

Lear: Ingrateful as they were, my heart feels yet
A pang of nature for their wretched Fall.
But, Edgar, I defer thy joys too long.
Thou served distressed Cordelia, take her crowned.
The imperial grace fresh blooming on her brow.
Nay, Gloster, thou hast here a father's right
Thy helping hand to heap blessings on their head.

Kent: Old Kent throws in his hearty wishes too.

Edgar: The Gods and you too largely recompense
What I have done. The gift strikes merit dumb.

Cordelia: Nor do I blush to own my self overpaid
For all my sufferings past.

Gloster: Now, gentle Gods, give Gloster his discharge.

Lear: No, Gloster, thou hast business yet for life.
Thou, Kent, and I, retired to some cool cell
Will gently pass our short reserves of Time.
In calm reflections on our fortunes past,
Cheered with relation of the prosperous reign
Of this celestial pair. Thus our remains
Shall in an even course of thought be past,
Enjoy the present hour, nor fear the last.

Edgar: Our drooping country now erects her head,
Peace spreads her balmy wings, and plenty blooms.
Divine Cordelia, all the gods can witness
How much thy love to empire I prefer!
Thy bright example shall convince the world
(Whatever storms of fortune are decreed)
That truth and virtue shall at last succeed.

Exit all

A NOVEL PERSPECTIVE: JANE SMILEY'S *A THOUSAND ACRES*

In 1991, American novelist Jane Smiley wrote *A Thousand Acres.* Her novel is a twentieth-century American version of *King Lear,* set on a farm in the Midwestern United States. But Smiley has changed more than just the time and place of the story and the genre in which it is told. She has also changed the point of view. The story is told from the perspective of the eldest daughter, Ginny (Goneril), and she and her sister Rose (Regan), are portrayed in a much more sympathetic manner. Their father, Larry Cook (Lear), is an irritable, difficult man who decides to divide the farm among his adult daughters in order to avoid inheritance taxes. His irrational, unpredictable behavior seems to suggest that he may be suffering from Alzheimer's or some other form of dementia. But before we can begin to feel too much sympathy for him, we learn that he has a history of beating and molesting his daughters. Indeed, Rose resents that fact that his dementia makes him an object of sympathy for the neighbors and prevents him from ever realizing what he has done to his daughters. In light of his abuse of his daughters, Ginny and Rose's anger and resentment is understandable, and because of his dementia, their treatment of him, which is never as extreme as Goneril and Regan's treatment of Lear, seems understandable. It seems reasonable, and even responsible for adult daughters to limit the freedom of an aged father whose dementia is causing him to drive drunk and to spend large sums of money carelessly. Even Caroline (Cordelia), seems much less agreeable in her support of her father. Rather than appearing as the one true, loyal daughter, she seems to be the one daughter who has escaped abuse and who doesn't truly understand who her father or sisters are.

In spite of these major changes, however, the parallels to the original plot are striking. Larry does divide his farm, and he cuts Caroline out because she has "spoken as a lawyer when she should have spoken as a daughter" (*A Thousand Acres* [New York: Ballantine, 1992], 21). Larry does curse his daughters with infertility, just as Lear asks the goddess Nature to "dry up in [Goneril] the organs of increase" (1.4.256) and we see Larry's curse carried out in Ginny's miscarriages and Rose's breast cancer, both caused by the poisoned well water on the farm. Larry does wander out into the storm after cursing his daughters, and Caroline cannot forgive them for this even though she is told that her sisters tried to stop him and tried to take him home. Howard (Gloucester) is blinded in a farming accident that is in fact caused by Pete (Cornwall). Larry and Caroline do attempt, unsuccessfully, to recover the farm. And Rose and Ginny, who have been very close throughout their lives, do both fall in love with Jess Clark (Edmund), which leads Ginny to attempt to poison Rose.

But naturally, since it is Ginny, and not Larry, with whom we sympathize, it is also Ginny, and not her father, who has the revelations and recognition typical of a tragic hero. She is only one of the many characters who suffers a tragic reversal of fortunes, but she is the only character in the novel who recognizes her own faults and her own role in her tragedy. In the final pages of the novel she inventories what she calls her inheritance, the lessons she has learned from the people she has known, and finally she lists what she learned from her own horrific attempt to poison her sister:

I remember my dead young self, who left me something, too, which is her canning jar of poisoned sausage and the ability it confers, of remembering what you can't imagine. I can't say that I forgive my father, but now I can imagine what he probably chose never to remember—the goad of an unthinkable urge, pricking him, pressing him, wrapping him in an impenetrable fog of self that must have seemed, when he wandered around the house late at night after working and drinking, like the very darkness. This is the gleaming obsidian shard I safeguard above all the others. (*A Thousand Acres*, 370–1)

Ginny does not forgive her father at the end of the novel, but she recognizes that both she and her father have been capable of thinking and doing unimaginable, horrible things. Like Lear, she confronts her own flaws and admits to her tragic mistakes. Her father, incapacitated by both dementia and his own ego, never faces or confronts his own failures as a farmer or as a father.

SMILEY'S *A THOUSAND ACRES*

In the following book review, Ron Carlson attempts, somewhat unsuccessfully, to avoid comparing Jane Smiley's *A Thousand Acres* to Shakespeare's *King Lear*. He observes that while there are many similarities, the book "doesn't lean against *Lear* for support." This is an interesting point to consider. To what extent is an adaptation its own work? To what extent is it an adaptation merely "an exercise, . . . some clever, layered construct"? Ideally, an adaptation should be in dialogue with the original text. They should both comment on and shed light on one another. The fact that Mr. Carlson cannot avoid references to *King Lear* when talking about *A Thousand Acres* suggests that Jane Smiley has been successful in creating this dialogue. If, as Carlson notes, the book reminds us why *King Lear* has lasted, asks some of the same questions about family bonds posed by *King Lear,* and yet creates a very realistic setting and engaging characters which are quite different from those of *King Lear,* then Smiley has succeeded in writing a novel that is both its own work and a work engaged in an interesting dialogue with Shakespeare's play.

FROM RON CARLSON, KING LEAR IN ZEBULON COUNTY

By Ron Carlson. *New York Times* 1991. Copyright © November 3, 1991, *The New York Times.* Reprinted by permission.

It is hard to resist comparing Jane Smiley's big new novel, "A Thousand Acres," to "King Lear," but I'm going to try. Does an imperious and domineering father divide his domain and leave the youngest of his three daughters out? Does this lead beyond mayhem to tragedy? Is someone blinded? Is there a storm? Well, yes, and a dozen other yeses, but this powerful and poignant book doesn't lean against Lear for support. Jane Smiley takes the truths therein and lights them up her way, making the perils of family and property and being a daughter real and personal and new and honest and hurtful all over again. And where? In Iowa.

A farm of a thousand acres is a magnificent thing. Certainly Larry Cook's place stands as one of the largest landholdings in Zebulon County. Amassed in deals that arose from his neighbors' failures, the farm is a tribute to Larry Cook's single-minded shrewdness.

It is May of 1979, and when a neighbor, Harold Clark, holds a community pig roast to announce the return of his prodigal son, Jess, Larry Cook uses the occasion to announce—surprisingly—that he is giving his farm to his daughters: Ginny, Rose and Caroline. At the last minute, angered by her seeming hesitance, he cuts Caroline, the youngest, out of the grant. Those rich and fertile thousand acres will do more damage to a family than any real estate since the cherry orchard.

Ginny Cook narrates the book from her position as the oldest daughter, 36 that year; but in so many ways she is the youngest, the most callow, the slowest to judge. This is one of Ms. Smiley's finest strokes, the selection of her storyteller. For Ginny is neutral, without agenda, at times as stolid as a farm animal—almost reluctantly drawn into the events of the summer, events that will force her into discovering the true nature of her family and her past.

It's Ginny's strange innocence that accompanies us through the novel and lends the story a marvelous and personal tension so credible it is chilling. She's the kind of person who, despite lingering sadness at being childless after several miscarriages, is still perked up by the sight of the colors of a Monopoly board. She is married to Ty Smith, a good farmer, an orderly and blameless man. She is also the caretaker of the group; at the time the novel opens, she's cooking breakfast in three houses—hers, her father's and her sister Rose's. Rose, at 34, is recovering from a mastectomy.

Ginny's sisters are already more worldly wise than she. Rose has always been a realist, holding her emotions at arm's length. She says of her grandfather and father on the farm: "First their wives collapse under the strain, then they take it out on their children for as long as they can." She has kept score and lives for retribution. When her husband, Pete, broke her arm four years before, she made a sleeve for the cast that said, "PETE DID THIS." Rose and Pete live with their two daughters across the road from her father.

Only Caroline, 28, has escaped her father's world; she has become, along with her husband, Frank, a lawyer in Des Moines. The youngest, the prettiest, the most successful, Caroline was raised by her sisters after her mother's death. It is her "I don't know" when the question of returning to the farm first arises that labels her a thankless child. Larry Cook has never been a tolerant man.

He has also never been a man for whom anything but the land really mattered, and giving up the farm that was his life unmoors him. In what was supposed to be his retirement, he becomes a quarrelsome wanderer, setting off a series of events that leads to a tempestuous denouement. Typically, one of the first of these events is seemingly unimportant: buying new kitchen cabinets that sit where the delivery men left them, out in his yard unprotected from the weather, like a beacon to the community—something is wrong. His sullen idleness, his drinking, his smoldering anger lead him down a path of accident and rancor, from Ginny to Rose to his best friend, Harold Clark, to Caroline and finally to court. He can't talk, but he can curse.

As the Cooks' problems intensify, a stranger comes to town. Jess Clark, who went to Canada during the Vietnam War, has returned after several years. For Ginny and Rose, he's a welcome addition to the community, and in a wonderful early scene a marathon game of Monopoly becomes a way of exchanging news, about everything from Jess's views on organic farming to what is being said in town about Larry Cook's daughters. Jess's involvement with Ginny and Rose becomes the key to Ginny's awakening to herself, to her full understanding of Rose.

Jane Smiley knows that the forces at play in any rural society are powerful and not unsophisticated. There is nature to contend with. There's the housewives' constant struggle to keep the farm out of the house. And there is the rivalry of farmer against farmer, the competition for success with the crops, with machinery and with the bank—which ends sometimes in vying for one another's farms. Ginny remembers her father looking across the road at the Ericsons' place. "We might as well have had a catechism," she says. "What is a farmer's first duty? To grow more food. What is a farmer's second duty? To buy more land." Larry Cook closed the Ericson deal on the day of his wife's funeral.

Ms. Smiley's portrait of the American farm is so vivid and immediate—the way farmers walk, what the corn looks like, the buzz of conversation at the community dinners—that it causes a kind of stunning nostalgia. It reminds us that the passing on of farms is always difficult—and that the farmer's inherent character makes it even more so. The distance from the main house to the son's or daughter's across the road is one of the most tangible embodiments of the generation gap.

And all these struggles are played out under the gaze of the community. The flat farmland is a fishbowl. For miles one can see whose crops are thriving, whose barn is painted, whose car is headed for town or returning and at what hour. Jane Smiley's townsfolk—the bankers, neighbors and family friends—are the Greek chorus here. In fact, there is something fundamentally Midwestern about a chorus, about all that caution. The community is slow to change, hardly warm to Larry Cook's decision.

There are surprises in this book, things to be uncovered, events that turn in ways more radical and permanent than we would have supposed. When sister talks to sister in the kitchen or on the phone or in the courtroom, Ms. Smiley brings us in so close that it's almost too much to bear. She's good in those small spaces, with nothing but the family, pulling tighter and tighter until someone has to leave the table, leave the room, leave town. And she's good in the big spaces—this region is hers now, intuited and understood, and delivered with generous exactitude. Ms. Smiley's earlier work—including the novellas "Ordinary Love & Good Will" and the story collection "The Age of Grief"—has been praised by the literary world. But "A Thousand Acres" is the big book that will finally earn her the wider audience she deserves.

I was reluctant, in writing about the novel, to invoke "King Lear" (and it will be invoked, believe me) because I didn't want this story to sound like an exercise, like some clever, layered construct. What "A Thousand Acres" does is to remind us again of why "King Lear" has lasted.

This is a book about farming in America, the loss of family farms, the force of the family itself. It is intimate and involving. What, Ms. Smiley asks, is it to be a true daughter? And what is the price to be paid for trying one's whole life to please a proud father who only slenderly knows himself—who coveted his land the way he loved his daughters, not wisely but too too well?

A THOUSAND ACRES—THE FILM

Six years after the publication of Smiley's novel, director Jocelyn Moorhouse adapted Smiley's adaptation of *King Lear* into a film. Her film tells essentially the same story as Smiley's book, though the visual medium of film allows for the connection between Larry Cook and his farm to be made even clearer.

As the film progresses, Larry becomes a rather minor character, disappearing into the background, but shots of the rolling landscape continue to fill the film. The land takes Larry's place and dominates the film as Larry dominated his daughters.

But the most notable difference between the film and the novel lies in the absence of any evil in Ginny. In the film, Ginny never attempts to poison her sister, and therefore she cannot have the same tragic revelation at the end of the film. She never acknowledges her own contributions to her tragic "inheritance," and indeed, in the film, her inheritance is less tragic. In place of Ginny's inventory of her inheritance, the film ends with Ginny's optimistic voiceover:

> Although the farm and all of its gifts and burdens are scattered now, my inheritance is with me in Rose's children. As each year goes by, I watch them grow, and in them I see something new, something my sister and I never had. I see hope.

The film ends on a more positive note than either Smiley's novel or Shakespeare's play, but it also eliminates the tragic recognition that the heroes of both those works experience. Moorhouse's Ginny does not see her own faults; she sees only hope. In this sense, Moorhouse's film revises Smiley's novel in much the same way that Tate revised Shakespeare's *King Lear*. It emphasizes the issues of incest, abuse, the damage they cause, and the possibility of recovery, but it does not emphasize, as the novel does, the possibility of growing and learning from the recognition of one's own faults and tragic flaws.

MOORHOUSE'S *A THOUSAND ACRES*

The following film review, like Ron Carlson's review of Smiley's novel, raises questions about the role of an adaptation and its relation to the original text. Russell Smith suggests that "The best way to appreciate this film is to ignore the contrived Shakespearean parallels and savor the skill with which Moorhouse undermines the conventions of the heartland family drama." It may be, however, that the undermining of a heartland family drama is, in fact, one of the strongest Shakespearean parallels in the film. The film, like both Shakespeare's play and Smiley's novel, raises questions about the family roles, the ties that bind families together, and the acts that can sever those ties. As you read this review and watch the film, consider whether you think the film successfully enters into dialogue with *King Lear*. Does watching Jocelyn Moorhouse's *A Thousand Acres* help you to understand *King Lear* in new ways?

Larry Cook (Jason Robards) rages at his daughters Ginny (Jessica Lange) and Rose (Michelle Pfeiffer) in Jocelyn Moorhouse's *A Thousand Acres*. Reprinted with permission of Photofest.

FROM RUSSELL SMITH, FILM REVIEW OF
A THOUSAND ACRES

By Russell Smith. September 22, 1997, *The Austin Chronicle*

Jane Smiley's Pulitzer Prize-winning, Lear-on-a-John Deere novel has reached the screen with its bleak and anguished spirit intact. That's a bit of a surprise considering that the last outing for Australian director Jocelyn Moorhouse was the maudlin *How to Make an American Quilt*. But go back to her debut film, the minor masterpiece Proof, and the artistic marriage makes a lot more sense. As that dark little jewel proved, Moorhouse knows plenty about pain, betrayal, and damaged souls... all of which figure prominently in Smiley's transplantation of Shakespeare's tragedy to the Iowa cornfields. Lear is reincarnated here as Larry Cook (Robards), a flinty old farmer who connives to avoid inheritance taxes by incorporating his business and dividing it among daughters Rose (Pfeiffer), Ginny (Lange) and Caroline (Leigh). Youngest daughter Caroline, our Cordelia figure, gets stripped of her inheritance, however, when she confesses doubts about the scheme. Soon thereafter, the old man starts sinking into a mire of boozing, depression, and senility. Ginny has an adulterous affair with a neighbor (Firth), and terrible family secrets start emerging in conversations between the two elder daughters, played with exquisitely controlled intensity by Lange and Pfeiffer. Caroline, a big-city lawyer, avails herself of the chaos to re-ingratiate herself with Larry by supporting his effort to nullify the land transfer. Smiley's story, adapted by Laura Jones, doesn't hew slavishly to Shakespeare. The key difference is that Larry, unlike Lear, isn't a victim of literal or figurative blindness, or the evil of others. Instead, he is evil incarnate, lacking only cloven hoofs and leathery wings. Caroline is an unwitting accomplice, not a wronged innocent like Cordelia, and Larry's raging-in-the-storm scene is ugly, harrowing, and utterly lacking any of Lear's mad eloquence. The best way to appreciate this film is to ignore the contrived Shakespearean parallels and savor the skill with which Moorhouse undermines the conventions of the heartland family drama. Dreamy early images of ripening grain and Robards' noble, marble-bust visage combine with a lullaby score to place the viewer in one of Hollywood's all-too-familiar Places in the Heart. Then, a trap door drops and you plummet into icy, stygian darkness where the dominant smell is sulfur, not simmering rhubarb pie. This is a hard, angry, morally unforgiving movie with dominant sensibilities more similar to the current wave of "therapy fiction" than to the classical tragedy genre. Superimposing these raw, primal emotions onto amber-hued scenes of bucolic splendor creates a satisfying tension that sustains interest even when the story veers uncomfortably close to primetime soap territory. Though not a completely successful film, *A Thousand Acres* is hard-hitting, original, and brimming with unwavering moral convictions and the courage to follow them to their troubling conclusions.

RAN

In 1985, renowned film director, Akira Kurosawa, directed *Ran,* an adaptation of *King Lear* set in sixteenth-century Japan. The word *ran* means *chaos* in Japanese, and indeed, the film depicts a kingdom crumbling into chaos. Like Lear, Lord Hidetora Ichimonji decides to give his kingdom to his children so that he can enjoy his old age without the worries of the kingdom. Unlike Lear, Hidetora has three sons, and he gives the kingdom to his eldest son, Taro, while he gives the second and third castles to his two younger sons, Jiro and Saburo, asking them to support their elder brother. Taro and Jiro praise and flatter their father, but Saburo criticizes him and tells him he is either mad or senile to depend on the fidelity or unity of his sons, who have grown up in a "world barren of loyalty and feeling" and who have seen their father mercilessly shed blood in order to maintain power. When Lord Hidetora hands his sons three arrows, bundled together, to show them how the three of them together will be indestructible, Saburo breaks the three arrows over his knees and calls his father a senile old fool. Enraged, Lord Hidetora cuts Saburo out and banishes a faithful servant, Tango, who criticizes his decision. Saburo's predictions of war and disloyalty quickly come to pass. The two elder sons cast out their father and turn on each other.

Although Hidetora has sons, and not daughters, the role of the malevolent, evil woman is not missing from the film. Lady Kaede, originally the wife of Taro and then, after his death, the consort of Jiro, is as devious and malicious as Regan and Goneril combined. After Lord Hidetora resigns his power, she reveals that he had murdered her family and that the first castle, in which she and Taro now live, was her family castle. She is bent on revenge against the Ichimonji family. She first insults Hidetora by refusing to step out of the way for his concubines. Then she convinces Taro to take back the insignia and banners that Hidetora had taken with him, and gradually she erodes the rights and privileges that Hidetora has attempted to retain. Finally, he is driven out of his castle. When Taro is killed in battle, Lady Kaede seduces Jiro, and then insists that he kill his current wife, Lady Sue, and bring her Lady Sue's head. Kurogane, Jiro's servant, refuses to kill Lady Sue and instead brings Kaede the head of a statue of a fox. He tells Jiro that many foxes take the form of women, and he warns him to beware of such women. At the end of the film, Lady Kaede confesses that she wanted to destroy the Ichimonji family and wanted to see the castle burn. Kurogane beheads her, and leads Jiro out to a battle that will surely result in their death, but Kaede has already succeeded in destroying Hidetora's family and kingdom.

Kaede's cruelty stands in stark contrast to the gentle spirit of Sue and her brother, Tsurumaru. Although their family was also murdered by Lord Hidetora, Sue is not vengeful, a fact that causes Hidetora much guilt. Her brother, whose eyes were gouged out by Hidetora, is more resentful than his sister, but he strives to be like her and to meditate on Buddha. When Hidetora and his fool are wandering, lost and mad, they seek refuge in Tsurumaru's house, and he declares, "lacking anything else, I will give you hospitality of the heart."

Hidetora's fool, Kyoami, plays as important a role in this film as Lear's fool did in Shakespeare's play. Like Lear's fool, Kyoami teases his master and tells him how foolish he has been, but he also loyally follows his master as Lord Hidetora wanders in the wilderness and descends into madness. Although tempted to leave his master, he cannot bring himself to do it. Whereas the Fool in Shakespeare's play disappears (or has no speaking part), after act three, the fool in Kurosawa's film stays with Hidetora until Hidetora runs off in a fit of madness and fear, and then Kyoami finds Saburo and helps him to find his father again.

After finding his father and convincing him that he does not want to kill him, Saburo rides back to his army with his father seated behind him on his horse. As they ride, Hidetora says to his son, "I have so much to say. When we are alone and quiet we will talk, father to son. That's all I want." It is a moving scene, reminiscent of Lear's scene of reconciliation with Cordelia, but it is cut short when Saburo is shot by one of his brother's soldiers. As Hidetora kneels at the side of his dead son, he grieves the injustice of this death, and struggles, like Lear, to accept the reality of such a sudden, tragic loss. He speaks to his dead son and says, "You can't die. I have tales to tell, forgiveness to ask.

Lord Hidetora (Tatsuya Nakadai) with his loyal Fool, Kyoami (Peter) in Akira Kurosawa's *Ran*. Reprinted with permission of Photofest.

Is this justice? Are you gone forever?" Like Lear, Hidetora dies of grief, wailing and collapsing on top of his son's corpse. Upon seeing his master dead, the fool, Kyoami, begins to weep like a child, to beg Hidetora not to die, and to curse the gods for their cruelty. Tango, however, tells him not to "call back his spirit" because he has suffered enough, and he tells him not to blame the gods: "It is the gods who weep. They see us killing each other over and over since time began. They can't save us from ourselves." His speech is a reminder that it is human failures that have caused this tragedy. The final scene of the film shows the blind Tsurumaru alone at the brink of a cliff. His sister has been killed, and with no one left to guide him, he is far more helpless than Gloucester was at his imaginary cliff. He clutches a picture of Buddha, which his sister left with him, but as he takes a cautious step forward and feels the edge of the cliff, he panics and drops the picture. Now he is utterly alone. Kurosawa's film leaves even fewer survivors than Shakespeare's play, and there seems little hope for the rebuilding of this kingdom.

KUROSAWA'S *RAN*

In David Ng's review of *Ran,* which follows, he focuses on the motifs of duplicity, hypocrisy, and deception in the film. Things are not what they seem. Characters present one outer appearance, but then prove to be something very different. The film, likewise, "seems to be one thing but soon proves itself infinitely complex." *Ran,* Ng notes, "ultimately subverts the values it so deceptively inhabits." This pattern of duplicity and hypocrisy also runs through Shakespeare's *King Lear.* The flattering speeches of Regan and Goneril prove to be worthless, while the stark, bare speech of Cordelia proves to be a valuable proclamation of love. As you read David Ng's review, consider whether you think Kurosawa has placed more emphasis than Shakespeare did on the idea that things are not what they seem. Does Shakespeare's play itself enter into this duplicity, as Ng claims that *Ran* does? Do you think that *King Lear,* like *Ran,* is a work "whose outward richness seduces us into thoroughly enjoying a tale of human damnation"?

FROM DAVID NG, REVIEW OF *RAN*

By David Ng. November 18, 2001 *Images*
http://www.imagesjournal.com/issue09/reviews/ran/

Akira Kurosawa's *Ran* is that rare epic picture, at once enormous and intimate, simultaneously melodramatic and nuanced. The superlatives that seem permanently attached to its name (magnificent, grand, breathtaking) betray its very nature: this is a quietly pessimistic movie, one that peels back the layers of deceit in its characters to find a Godless universe. Weaving together momentum and stasis, Kurosawa fashions a nimble motif of juxtaposition. Visual formality masks emotional anarchy. Like so many of its characters, *Ran* seems to be one thing but soon proves itself infinitely complex. The title translates to 'chaos' and true to its name, *Ran* ultimately subverts the values it so deceptively inhabits.

On the occasion of its 15th anniversary, Winstar Cinema is re-releasing *Ran* in a brand new 35mm print. Struck from a well-preserved negative stored in producer Serge Silberman's personal archive, *Ran* will tour the major U.S. cities before being widely released. This is a perfect opportunity for young filmgoers who've only seen the movie on video. Size does matter if we are to fully appreciate Kurosawa's characters at play in the fields of the Lord. In a strange way, Ran is also the ideal millennial movie. It ties together such big concepts as God and family in a story that, while ostensibly lifted from King Lear, plunges deeper into time by borrowing heavily from ancient Japanese fables and legends.

Ran follows Shakespeare's five act structure, but it feels more naturalistic than that. The first hour or so blows over us like a warm breeze. We meet Hidetora (Tatsuya Nakadai), an aging warlord, as he divides his kingdom among his three sons. The youngest, Saburo, rejects his inheritance and is banished. The elder two assume power in what Hidetora mistakenly believes to be a peaceful transition. Kurosawa composes these early scenes as a sequence of static shots, each of which are as detailed and inert as a painting. Setting these scenes amid vast mountains and the big sky reduces the characters to mere specks. All this fussing and quarrelling is inconsequential, Kurosawa suggests. What endures is the world around us.

The movie then moves inside, introducing us to a painfully ritualistic society in which people move and talk in slow motion. The rooms are spartan and feel two-dimensional. Kurosawa is imitating theater, creating an artificial world of symmetry and visual order. But it's the destruction of that outward perfection that interests Kurosawa and he wastes no time in introducing one of cinema's great bitches, Lady Kaide (Mieko Harada), wife of Taro, the eldest son. In her oppressively layered costumes, which themselves suggest mounds of duplicity, she orchestrates the banishment of Hidetora from his kingdom and instigates a war between the brothers. Lady Kaide may have wandered in from the set of MacBeth (or Kurosawa's own Throne of Blood) but she is a product of Japan's Noh theater: her makeup represents the face of remorseless Vengeance. Mourning the death of her husband later in the movie, she impassively crushes a butterfly between her fingers.

Hidetora's other daughter-in-law, Lady Sue, is a devout Buddhist and faithful subject, even though Hidetora once ravaged her home and blinded her brother. She has chosen forgiveness, which Hidetora can't understand. She, like his sons, behaves contrary to what he expects. Interestingly, her face is never shown, nor that of her brother's. They are spirit-like, floating somewhere above the political maneuverings. That Lady Sue and Lady Kaide should meet the same grisly fate points to a resigned atheism. Nothing is rewarded and everything is punished in a world devoid of divine intervention.

And yet God is everywhere in this movie. He's certainly in the battle scenes, which Kurosawa has filmed with a kind of omniscient detachment. He's also in the weather—gentle at first, then increasingly stormy as brother fights brother, and ultimately hurricane force as Hidetora goes insane and wanders the wilderness with his Fool. This is all punctuated by large, billowing clouds that Kurosawa frequently cuts to as if to emphasize the immateriality of it all. Clouds finally give way to a red sunset as the death toll mounts and we are left with complete destruction in the movie's final scenes. But nowhere is God's presence more apparent (and sorrowful) than in Hidetora's wizened face. Reason having long since abandoned him, his skin becomes chalky white, his beard long and unkempt, his face completely slack. He has grown confused by his own creation run amok and has lost the ability, and desire, to control it.

Ran was not Kurosawa's last film, but if feels like it. It's a movie about an old man, made by an old man, both of whom were weary of the world. At one point, Hidetora remarks, "How hard it is to be old!" For Kurosawa, the difficulty was in reconciling the hypocrisies he saw around him. Of his movie Rashomon, he wrote in his autobiography, "human beings are unable to be honest with themselves about themselves...even the character who dies cannot give up his lies." This cynicism informs Ran's ideology: who can endure a world where God is present but powerless, where family members betray each other, where insanity is the only means of survival? Enshrining the story in a sumptuous visual style, Kurosawa has perhaps created the ultimate social critique—a movie whose outward richness seduces us into thoroughly enjoying a tale of human damnation.

QUESTIONS FOR WRITTEN AND ORAL DISCUSSION

1.   Nahum Tate revised Shakespeare's play to suit the popular tastes of his time. Imagine that you are directing a Hollywood blockbuster version of *King Lear*. What changes would you make to the play? Why? What would the audience prefer about your version? Would you make any of the same changes that Tate made?

2.   In Tate's version of *King Lear,* Cordelia intentionally angers her father because she wants him to disinherit her. Does this alteration make her behavior seem more or less believable? Do you find it easier to believe that Cordelia refused to flatter and lie to her father even though it meant losing her inheritance? Or do you find it easier to accept that Cordelia wanted to anger her father so that she would lose the kingdom and escape an unwanted marriage?

3.   Tate says that he wanted to avoid a tragic ending that "encumbered the stage with dead bodies, which conduct makes many tragedies conclude with unseasonable jests." Do you think Shakespeare's play concludes with "unseasonable jests" or inappropriate humor? Do you think Tate's play concludes with "unseasonable jests"? Does turning the tragic ending into a happy ending make the ending comedic, or does it provide the play with a more serious, dignified ending, as Tate suggests?

4.   At the end of Tate's play, Lear regains his crown and then gives it away to Cordelia. Lear's earlier decision to give away his crown to his three daughters is generally seen as a mistake. Is it still a mistake at the end of Tate's play? Does it suggest that Lear has learned nothing? Or is it an appropriate ending since Cordelia has proven herself to be the most loyal and deserving daughter?

5.   Rewrite a scene of *King Lear* in prose, telling it from the point of view of one character. How, for instance, does the Fool describe the scene in the hovel? How does Lear describe the same scene? Kent? Edgar (Poor Tom)? Compare your rewrite with those of classmates who have rewritten the same scene from a different point of view. What do the different perspectives reveal about the scene?

6.   Compare the scene of *King Lear* in which Lear is turned out into the storm, act two, scene four, with the same scene in the novel *A Thousand Acres,* chapter twenty three. How are the scenes similar? How are they different? With whom do you sympathize in each case? Does reading this scene in the novel or seeing it in the film version of *A Thousand Acres* cause you to rethink your ideas about this scene in the play?

7.   Compare the final scene of Tate's *King Lear* with the final scene of Shakespeare's *King Lear.* The obvious difference is that Tate's version ends happily. What other dif-

ferences can you detect? Why might Tate have made these changes? What similarities do you see? Why might Tate have kept these portions of Shakespeare's play?

8. The film review of *A Thousand Acres* suggests that Jocelyn Moorhouse's film is more akin to a soap opera than to a Shakespearean tragedy. Do you agree? In what ways does the film resemble a soap opera? In what ways does it resemble a Shakespearean tragedy? Does *King Lear* resemble a soap opera?

9. In *Ran,* Lord Hidetora is guilty of murdering and torturing people to get his power. In Shakespeare's *King Lear,* we are told that Lear has neglected his people, taking "too little care" of the poor and needy, but we are never told that he has killed or tortured to gain power. Indeed, it is Cornwall and Goneril, not Lear, who gouge out Gloucester's eyes, whereas in *Ran* it is Lord Hidetora who has gouged out the eyes of Tsurumaru. Do these acts of violence make Hidetora a better or worse tragic hero? Refer to the definition of a tragic hero given in chapter one as you form your answer.

10. Kyoami, Lord Hidetora's fool, stays with Hidetora throughout the film, and grieves Hidetora's death in the final scene. In contrast, Lear's fool disappears, or at least stops speaking after act three of *King Lear.* How does the presence of the fool in the latter part of the film affect *Ran?* Does his presence serve a useful purpose? How would the film be affected if Kyoami, like Lear's fool, had disappeared halfway through the film?

11. Jane Smiley sets her version of *King Lear* on a farm in the American Midwest in the twentieth century, and in doing so she comments on incest, abuse, Alzheimer's, and farming practices. Kurosawa set his adaptation of *King Lear* in sixteenth-century Japan, and his film ends with an anti-war message. If you were going to write an adaptation of *Lear* in which you changed the time and place in which it was set, what setting would you use? Where and when would your adaptation take place? How would this setting be appropriate for the story? What would be gained from retelling the story in this way? On what new issues would this adaptation shed light? What aspects of Shakespeare's play still seem relevant in this new setting?

12. Compare the final scene of Shakespeare's *King Lear* with the final scene of Kurosawa's *Ran.* In what ways are the endings similar? How do they differ? Does either ending seem more tragic than the other? If so, what makes it more tragic?

13. This chapter has examined adaptations that changed the ending of the play, added love stories, changed the setting, changed the language, changed the genre, and altered the perspective of Shakespeare's play. Sketch some ideas for your own adaptation of *King Lear.* What will you change and why? What will you preserve and why? Prepare to present your ideas to the class.

6

Contemporary Application: Treatment of the Elderly

Writers of conduct books in Shakespeare's day stressed the responsibility of adult children to care for their elderly and ailing parents as their parents had cared for them when they were young, but the case of Sir Brian Annesley and his daughters, mentioned in chapter one, illustrates that caring for the elderly was not always a duty that children bore willingly or well. The treatment and mistreatment of the elderly is also an important issue in *King Lear*. Cordelia, seeing how her sisters have mistreated Lear, says, "Had you not been their father, these white flakes / Had challenged pity of them" (4.7.30–1). Lear, she argues, deserves the pity and respect of his daughters not only because he is their father but also because his white hair shows that he is a very old man. Gloucester, likewise, should have met with mercy from Regan both because he was her host and because his white beard, which she plucks, shows that he is an old man deserving of respect and sympathy. But even children far more dutiful and loving than Regan and Goneril can find caring for an elderly parent a difficult task.

The treatment of the elderly is as important an issue today as it was in Shakespeare's day. People tend to live longer than they did in the seventeenth century, but with an increased life span come increased problems. Alzheimer's disease and other causes of dementia, poor physical health, and separation from family members who live far away or who have little time to care for aging parents and grandparents are only a few of the problems faced by the elderly and their loved ones. Caring family members may find themselves overwhelmed by the financial, emotional, and physical burdens of caring for older relatives, and some of the elderly do not have family members to depend on. The following documents illustrate some of the many problems facing the elderly and their loved ones today and a few of the ways in which people choose to address these issues.

"THE INFIRMITY OF HIS AGE"

In the opening scene of *King Lear,* Lear announces that he wants to give up the burdens of being king, but he wants to retain the privileges that the position gives him. This was an absurd idea for a king in Shakespeare's time. Kings were given their power by God and they were expected to reign until their death. Regan and Goneril note his rash decision and see it as evidence that the "infirmity of his age" is affecting his judgment (1.1.291). Today, however, we might simply think of such an arrangement as a particularly nice retirement package. Many older Americans now look forward to a retirement during which they can relax and enjoy the fruits of their earlier years of work. But even modern Americans who can afford to retire and to give up their responsibilities can, like Lear, find their golden years dimmed by "the infirmity of...age." One form this infirmity can take is Alzheimer's disease, a disorder that causes a gradual loss of brain cells, leading to symptoms of dementia such as loss of memory, loss of reasoning skills, disorientation, agitation, and change in personality. Other diseases can cause similar symptoms in the elderly. The following two documents from the National Institute of Neurological Disorders and Stroke explain the symptoms of two common causes of dementia in the elderly, and they list the current prognoses and treatments for these disorders. In Shakespeare's day, of course, such treatments would not have been available. Rather, dementia might have been viewed as madness or insanity and treated with one of the methods described in chapter two. But these documents show that even today treatment of these disorders is limited. Often the only thing to be done is to treat the symptoms so as to make the patient more comfortable. As you read these documents, consider which of these symptoms you see in Lear's behavior.

FROM NATIONAL INSTITUTE OF NEUROLOGICAL DISORDERS AND STROKE, *NINDS ALZHEIMER'S INFORMATION PAGE*

National Institute of Neurological Disorders and Stroke, http:www.ninds.nih.gov/health_and_medical/disorders/alzheimersdisease_doc.htm (accessed September 10, 2003)

WHAT IS ALZHEIMER'S DISEASE?

Alzheimer's disease (AD) is a progressive, neurodegenerative disease characterized by memory loss, language deterioration, impaired visuospatial skills, poor judgment, indifferent attitude, but preserved motor function. AD usually begins after age 65, however, its onset may occur as early as age 40, appearing first as memory decline and, over several years, destroying cognition, personality, and ability to function. Confusion and restlessness may also occur. The type, severity, sequence, and progression of mental changes vary widely. The early symptoms of AD, which include forgetfulness and loss of concentration, can be missed easily because they resemble natural signs of aging. Similar symptoms can also result from fatigue, grief, depression, illness, vision or hearing loss, the use of alcohol or certain medications, or simply the burden of too many details to remember at once.

IS THERE ANY TREATMENT?

There is no cure for AD and no way to slow the progression of the disease. For some people in the early or middle stages of the disease, medication such as tacrine may alleviate some cognitive symptoms. Aricept (donepezil) and Exelon (rivastigmine) are reversible acetylcholinesterase inhibitors that are indicated for the treatment of mild to moderate dementia of the Alzheimer's type. Also, some medications may help control behavioral symptoms such as sleeplessness, agitation, wandering, anxiety, and depression. These treatments are aimed at making the patient more comfortable.

WHAT IS THE PROGNOSIS?

AD is a progressive disease. The course of the disease varies from person to person. Some people have the disease only for the last 5 years of life, while others may have it for as many as 20 years. The most common cause of death in AD patients is infection.

WHAT RESEARCH IS BEING DONE?

The NINDS conducts and supports research on neurodegenerative and dementing disorders, including AD. For example, although the cause of AD is still unknown, new research has shown that a vaccine, aimed at preventing or reversing the formation of AD-associated pathologic lesions, might be a useful therapy. Recent results using a transgenic mouse model suggest that immunological interventions may retard and even reverse the development of some of the pathologic changes associated with AD. Early clinical trials to test the vaccine are still in progress but offer hope for a future therapy. The National Institute on Aging and the National Institute of Mental Health also support research related to AD.

FROM NATIONAL INSTITUTE OF NEUROLOGICAL DISORDERS AND STROKE, *NINDS MULTI-INFARCT DEMENTIA INFORMATION PAGE*

National Institute of Neurological Disorders and Stroke,
http:www.ninds.nih.gov/health_and_medical/disorders/
multi-infarctdementia_doc.htm (accessed April 30, 2001)

WHAT IS MULTI-INFARCT DEMENTIA?

Multi-infarct dementia (MID), a common cause of dementia in the elderly, occurs when blood clots block small blood vessels in the brain and destroy brain tissue. Probable risk factors are high blood pressure and advanced age. CADASIL (cerebral autosomal dominant arteriopathy with subcortical infarcts and leukoencephalopathy) is an inherited form of MID. This disease can cause stroke, dementia, migraine-like headaches, and psychiatric disturbances. Symptoms of MID, which often develop in a stepwise manner, include confusion, problems with recent memory, wandering or getting lost in familiar places, loss of bladder or bowel control (incontinence), emotional problems such as laughing or crying inappropriately, difficulty following instructions, and problems handling money. Usually the damage is so slight that the change is noticeable only as a series of small steps. However over time, as more small vessels are blocked, there is a gradual mental decline. MID, which typically begins between the ages of 60 and 75, affects men more often than women.

IS THERE ANY TREATMENT?

Currently there is no treatment for MID that can reverse the damage that has already occurred. Treatment focuses on prevention of additional brain damage by controlling high blood pressure.

WHAT IS THE PROGNOSIS?

Prognosis for patients with MID is generally poor. Individuals with the disease may improve for short periods of time, then decline again. Early treatment and management of blood pressure may prevent further progression of the disorder.

WHAT RESEARCH IS BEING DONE?

The NINDS supports and conducts a wide range of research on dementing disorders such as MID and on cerebrovascular disease. The goals of this research are to improve the diagnosis of these disorders and to find ways to treat and prevent them.

AN AFFLICTED LEADER

Alzheimer's disease, which is one of the leading causes of dementia, was brought vividly to national attention in 1994 when ex-president Ronald Reagan wrote a letter to the American people announcing that he had Alzheimer's. In his letter, which follows, he speaks of his hope that announcing this publicly will raise public awareness, and he also talks of his desire to spend his retirement enjoyably with his wife. But he also predicts that much of the burden of the disease will fall on his family, and he regrets that.

Following his letter is an interview with Nancy Reagan, done in 2002. In it she admits that the ex-president has deteriorated quickly and that she is not even certain that he recognizes her. As you read these two documents, think of *King Lear,* and consider how this situation is similar. Does reading about the Reagans change the way you feel about either Lear or his daughters?

PRESIDENT RONALD REAGAN, LETTER TO THE AMERICAN PEOPLE (1994)

Nov. 5, 1994

My Fellow Americans,

I have recently been told that I am one of the millions of Americans who will be afflicted with Alzheimer's Disease.

Upon learning this news, Nancy & I had to decide whether as private citizens we would keep this a private matter or whether we would make this news known in a public way.

In the past Nancy suffered from breast cancer and I had my cancer surgeries. We found through our open disclosures we were able to raise public awareness. We were happy that as a result many more people underwent testing. They were treated in early stages and able to return to normal, healthy lives.

So now, we feel it is important to share it with you. In opening our hearts, we hope this might promote greater awareness of this condition. Perhaps it will encourage a clearer understanding of the individuals and families who are afflicted by it.

At the moment I feel just fine. I intend to live the remainder of the years God gives me on this earth doing the things I have always done. I will continue to share life's journey with my beloved Nancy and my family. I plan to enjoy the great outdoors and stay in touch with my friends and supporters.

Unfortunately, as Alzheimer's Disease progresses, the family often bears a heavy burden. I only wish there was some way I could spare Nancy from this painful experience. When the time comes I am confident that with your help she will face it with faith and courage.

In closing let me thank you, the American people for giving me the great honor of allowing me to serve as your President. When the Lord calls me home, whenever that may be, I will leave with the greatest love for this country of ours and eternal optimism for its future.

I now begin the journey that will lead me into the sunset of my life. I know that for America there will always be a bright dawn ahead.

Thank you, my friends. May God always bless you.

Sincerely,
Ronald Reagan

FORMER FIRST LADY ISN'T SURE FORMER PRESIDENT EVEN RECOGNIZES HER (2002)

The Associated Press State & Local Wire. *The Los Angeles Times,* September 24, 2002. Reprinted with the permission of the Associated Press.

Los Angeles

Ronald Reagan spends his days with advanced Alzheimer's disease secluded in his Bel-Air home under the care of wife Nancy, who isn't sure the former president even recognizes her.

In a CBS-TV "60 Minutes II" interview with longtime friend Mike Wallace, Mrs. Reagan said Alzheimer's has robbed the couple of their post-White House golden years. The interview at the Bel-Air Hotel will be broadcast Wednesday. "The golden years are when you can sit back, hopefully, and exchange memories, and that's the worst part about this disease: there's nobody to exchange memories with . . . and we had a lot of memories," Mrs. Reagan said.

Her 91-year-old husband's memory loss also takes the joy out of milestone occasions, like the couple's 50th wedding anniversary on March 4.

"I'd love to be able to talk to him about it, and there were times when I had to catch myself because I'd reach out and start to say, Honey, remember when?'" Mrs. Reagan said.

When asked by Wallace if her husband even knows who she is, she said, "I don't know."

Although Mrs. Reagan is visited regularly by daughter Patti Davis, the former first lady said she is lonely.

"Yes, it's lonely, because really, you know, when you come right down to it, you're in it alone and there's nothing that anybody can do for you, so it's lonely," Mrs. Reagan said.

The nation's 40th chief executive has only rarely been seen in public since his poignant 1994 letter announcing to the world that he had the memory-sapping disease.

Whenever asked about Reagan, his wife and chief of staff Joanne Drake say he's doing fine and leave it at that.

Twenty years ago, on Oct. 22, 1982, then-President Reagan called the newly formed Alzheimer's Association to the White House to sign a proclamation designating the first ever National Alzheimer's Awareness Week.

The Chicago-based association said Tuesday that it was the beginning of a revolution in awareness of, advocacy for, and insight into Alzheimer's disease.

AN AGING PARENT

The following is the first part of a three-part interview with James and Joyce, who are caring for Joyce's mother, Ella. Ella has exhibited symptoms of dementia, and has recently been diagnosed with Alzheimer's. This condition and other age-related health problems have made it impossible for Ella to continue living on her own, and she now resides in an assisted-living home near her daughter and son-in-law. In this first part of the interview, Joyce and James describe the symptoms of dementia that they have noticed in Ella, and the changes in her personality and behavior in recent years. Many of her symptoms are reminiscent of Lear's behavior. Just as Cordelia describes Lear as a "child-changed father" (4.7.17), Joyce describes her mother's behavior as childlike; just as the Fool tells Lear that he has "madest [his] daughters [his] mothers" (1.4.149–50), so Ella sometimes dreams that Joyce is her mother; and just as Lear loses his own identity and asks, "Does any here know me? This is not Lear" (1.4.201), so Ella's personality seems so changed that at times James wants to ask, "What have you done with Ella?" As you read this interview, look for these and other similarities, and consider how seeing Lear as an elderly man with Alzheimer's would affect your interpretation of the play.

AN INTERVIEW WITH ALZHEIMER'S CAREGIVERS: PART I

Interview conducted June 24, 2003, in Florence, Oregon.

When did you first start to notice symptoms of dementia in your mother, and what were the symptoms?

Joyce: She's always been maybe not real good in some things. Or a little bit...didn't have an aptitude for some things. I just never thought about some of these things as dementia. Now thinking back I can see. The first thing I really noticed that I was concerned enough about to take her to a doctor about, was when I took her to a store that she was very, very familiar with, her favorite health food store. And she couldn't find the department. In fact she went in exactly the opposite direction of the department that she was looking for. And she knew that store like the back of her hand and she was very familiar with it. And she couldn't find the right department, and she wasn't in the right place, and just the last time I'd taken her there she knew how to find it. It was just like something had happened. And I was concerned enough at that time that I took her to her doctor. And that's the first time her doctor gave her an I.Q. test, a test for dementia, asking her what year is this, who the president is, and all those things. She knew what year it was. She knew who the president was but she couldn't remember his name. She thought he was a geek. Most of her answers were pretty, you know, not bad, as far as the questions she was given at that time.

And what are her current symptoms? How has it changed?

Joyce: Currently, she gets her days and nights mixed up, gets which day of the week it is mixed up. I think she would still probably be able to answer most of the same questions that she was given then. They just didn't ask her the right questions. If she was given those same questions that she was asked then, I think she would still be able to answer most of them. But she now has for quite some time had trouble... for a long time when she went out the door of her apartment at the assisted-living home, she would go in the opposite direction of where she wanted to go to. She is not so bad about that now.

James: Except she tries to go into the kitchen.

Joyce: Yeah, when she leaves the dining room to go out, sometimes they find her trying to go into the kitchen to get back to her room. But she's just gone in the wrong direction.

James: I think you heard her today say, "That's a woman that I used to know in California, but she doesn't remember me." Well, the woman is not anyone who was ever in California, and of course she doesn't remember Ella

Joyce: Because she never knew her.

James: But to Ella this is Margaret, and Margaret just doesn't remember.

Joyce: Margaret says, "My name's Mildred." And after trying to tell her this quite a few times, I remembered what I have been told about therapeutic fibbing in a class I took.

What class was this?

Joyce: It was a caretakers class called, "Taking Care of You." And they touched a little bit on how to handle Alzheimer's people, not as much as I hope to get in the next class I take. But, the director at the assisted-living home reminded me of this, that instead of arguing about it I should just tell her something like, "Margaret has been ill, and that makes her confused so she doesn't remember you." It's hard for me to come up with things like this because I just was raised to always tell the truth, especially to my mother. And so I'm having a little difficulty coming up with things. It takes a little creativity to come up with things.

James: Now you asked the question to start with, when did we first notice this dementia and what were the symptoms. I don't think we really first noticed this and realized it was dementia until she had a few TIAs [transient ischemic attacks, (ministrokes)] and she had to come live in the assisted-living place near us. Before that she was living a couple of hours away from us, near her sisters, and so she had a lot of interaction with them. We would talk to her on the phone but we never really saw her. But even then she would get confused in her own apartment as to which direction her bedroom was. But we never associated that with dementia. We just thought she didn't have a good sense of direction. But when we look back on it, I can remember clear back in 1996 that she couldn't remember the name of onions. I took her shopping because she wasn't driving anymore so I took her to do her grocery shopping, and this was really hard on her because she never liked to make out a grocery list. She just was used to running to the store every day when she needed something, so buying her groceries once a week was difficult for her. So she would try to write down what she needed, but she had a hard time writing down certain things that she wanted. She knew what she wanted but she couldn't remember the name of it. But we really noticed it about two and a half years ago when she had these TIAs, and then we really noticed it when she had pneumonia.

Joyce: That was a big thing. When she got pneumonia, suddenly, she would have spells when she didn't recognize pictures of her own sister that she's closest to. I thought it would be something to do with her to keep her occupied. I showed her a picture of her sister she's so close to and said, "See, who this is?" and she didn't know.

James: Not too long ago Joyce went to see her, just to drop some stuff off, and I got a phone call from her, and she said, "There was a woman in my room and she said she's my daughter. Who do you suppose she was?" It was her daughter. That's when we were aware that there was some dementia. We were just under the assumption that it was age-related dementia. And we were almost told that by the staff at the assisted-living place because you can bring her out of it, as opposed to Alzheimer's. But when we took her to see a specialist, she thinks it is Alzheimer's. And yes, you can bring her out of it, but it just keeps gradually increasing and it has been for the last eight years.

When you say she mixes up her days and nights, what do you mean?

Joyce: They tell me, the head nurse tells me, that since the day we first brought her to the assisted-living place they find her walking down the halls fully dressed in the middle of the night, going down to breakfast, or asking "Where is everybody?" That's been a problem since day one, and she still does that. She will be convinced that she hasn't had breakfast yet when she has. She'll be convinced that it is time for breakfast when it is time for dinner. She'll be waiting at the rope. They don't let them into the dining hall because they need time to clean up. So they have a rope to keep people out, and she'll be waiting there. And when people tell her it's not mealtime, she thinks they are lying to her.

James: "They're trying to confuse me" is her term.

Joyce: And she thinks it is them that are not telling her the truth when they tell her that it's a different time of day, or she'll be convinced that it is Sunday, time for church. She'll call me up and say, "I'm ready for church. I want to go with you today."

James: And it will be Wednesday.

Joyce: Or Tuesday.

James: In the afternoon. She will call in the middle of the night, about 2:00 in the morning, and say, "I'm hungry. I can't seem to get anything to eat around here. Can you pick me up and take us to get something to eat?" And this was before I realized that she just couldn't comprehend the difference between night and day or what time it was. I just let her talk to Joyce, but after Joyce told her it was time for bed, go to bed, she apparently called her sister who said, "don't you ever look at the clock?" So then she called another sister.

Joyce: She was calling quite a few different people for a while. I think she's stopped doing that because I turned off the ringer in the bedroom because I just wasn't getting any sleep.

James: We finally had to turn the phone off in our bedroom and let the answering machine answer it in the kitchen. And for a while we'd have five or six messages each morning because she forgets she's already called.

Joyce: Or if we take off for the day, even if I tell her ahead of time, "We're going to be gone for the day." When I come back there are apt to be nine or ten or twelve messages, one right after another, saying, "Joyce, I can't get a hold of you." For a while she used to say, "Why don't you ever answer your phone? Why do you have a phone if you don't answer it?"

James: But you can tell by the timer on the phone that the messages are maybe two minutes apart, one after another. Sometimes I've answered the phone and she says, "Well I don't know where I am." And I said, "Well you must be in your room or you couldn't have called me." But at those particular times she just can't fathom where she is. It just doesn't work. There's a missing connection.

What changes have you noticed in your mother's personality or behavior in the last couple of years?

Joyce: She's much more, I don't want to say selfish, but most of the time I don't think she realizes how much of a burden she is. Like today, you saw, she really wanted to come with us. She didn't know where we were going, but she wanted to go with us, and yet she couldn't really participate in the conversation. She wasn't really talking to us. Her attention span is very short. She used to love to work crossword puzzles, but she can't work them anymore. They were always simple crossword puzzles, but she can't do that anymore. Even after her eyesight was fixed.

James: She has become very selfish, and that's not at all what she was like before. So sometimes I just want to shake her and ask, "What have you done with Ella?" She's become childlike, is the way I would describe it, and just as a child doesn't think about other relationships, she doesn't. And maybe I would be the same way if I were stuck in a wheelchair, and I couldn't walk and couldn't do this. I probably would tend to be the same way. But it makes it hard when you are trying to do something for somebody and you ask, "What would you like to do?" and she says, "Oh, whatever." That doesn't help.

Joyce: Yeah, she can't make decisions of any kind, really. If you ask her what she wants to do she wouldn't know. You almost have to make every decision for her, and that's very hard for me. I didn't even like making decisions for my children growing up. It's like raising a second family almost.

She told me one day, "I had a dream that you were my mother," and I said, "Well, sometimes I feel that way." But it is a reversal of roles. It's a complete reversal of roles.

I guess the main thing is, and this is hard on her, I can tell, and she has even mentioned this one time, but she was always a person that was taking care of other people. She was a caretaker, and now she's being taken care of. And it still seems to make her feel better if she can do something for somebody else.

She raised her children and took care of her husband who was an invalid and was always the person who drove other little old ladies to the grocery store or to church, and did meals- on-wheels.

Joyce: And even drove children to church past the time when she should have been driving anyone, which scared me to death.

In *King Lear* his daughters describe his behavior as "unruly waywardness." He's making poor judgments, and he's getting angry at people he has no reason to get angry at. Do you see that sort of behavior in your mother?

Joyce: Oh, well, yeah. She's not a person who is usually unkind or anything. But she would get mad at her caretakers because they tell her to go back to bed in the middle of the night. Or, when she called me up in the middle of the night and I tell her, "Mom, it's 2:00 A.M.," she thinks that's funny. She's embarrassed so she's laughing, but I feel like really yelling at her, so I don't answer the phone anymore.

James: Well, yes, I can say that there are times where you call her and she'll answer the phone and say, grumpily, "Yeah, what do you want?" And also she gets mad at you because you're not there when she thinks you should be there, not when you should be there. And I don't think she can tell time anymore.

Joyce: And she told another woman who has been riding with us over to the Alzheimer's respite classes, "Well, Joyce is late a lot, or else she doesn't come."

Which has to be frustrating when you are doing all you are.

Joyce: Yeah, it is, and she told her sister, a couple years ago, "Sometimes Joyce doesn't come to see me for four days at a time." And I had been going over there maybe several times a day. And that really did make me mad, really did hurt my feelings. But of course that was before I really realized what her problem was.

And recently there have been some problems with her being found in the parking lot or wandering off?

Joyce: Well, she hasn't wandered off yet. When we first moved her after Christmas, she was very confused about the move. Moving is very hard on older people, and it was very hard on her, and I knew it would be. And they found her off in the wrong hall several times. There is a sign on the door that says her name. One of the caretakers made that for her because she couldn't find her room so many times. She went into the wrong rooms several times, really upset some of the ladies, especially the one across the hall from her. She went in there in the middle of the night. And that woman isn't in a lot better shape than Mother, but she insists that her door is left open at night and her light on. So Mother just walked in to find someone to visit in the middle of the night. This concerned me because the two things that could possibly make them make her move from the assisted-living home are if she starts wandering around town in the middle of the night or if she starts invading other people's privacy and there's a complaint. But fortunately she seems to not be doing that anymore, going into other people's rooms. There have been two times that I know of where she went out into the outside. One was shortly after we moved her downstairs, and the other was just the other day, and I don't know what brought that on. When we first moved her downstairs, she got confused which door was the right door out. And so one of the caretakers found her at nighttime about to go out onto her patio, with the door open there. So, for the time being, I knew what was causing that. They thought she was trying to leave, but I knew she just didn't know which door to take, so I just moved a piece of furniture in front of the door, and now she doesn't do that anymore. That is a problem, wandering, that you worry about.

THE CAREGIVERS

When Jane Smiley wrote *A Thousand Acres,* her adaptation of *King Lear,* she told the story from the point of view of the eldest daughter, who is caring for a senile father who was previously abusive. In doing this she shifts our sympathics, allowing us to see things from Regan and Goneril's point of view, and emphasizing the difficulty of caring for an elderly parent. The articles that follow also highlight those difficulties, and they illustrate that whether or not the aging parents have Alzheimer's, it can be difficult for the adult children to care for their parents without compromising other parts of their lives. While Renaissance conduct books argued that children owed their parents "recompense" and needed to care for their elderly parents as their parents had cared for them, the following documents show how difficult that idea can be in practice.

In the following article, "Caring for a Parent—Did I Do Enough?" Beth Witrogen McLeod explores the feelings of guilt and inadequacy that caregivers often feel when they are not able to repay the parents who raised them by caring for them in their old age. While Regan, Goneril, and Edmund all fail to show "recompense" to their parents, it is possible that even the generous behavior of Cordelia and Edgar could eventually lead to guilt, frustration, and a living situation that is unhealthy for both parent and child.

BETH WITROGEN MCLEOD, "CARING FOR A PARENT—DID I DO ENOUGH?"

By Beth Witrogen McLeod. Copyright WebMD, Inc. 2000, June 19, 2000
http://my.webmd.com/content/article/11/1674_50512.htm?

(WebMD)—Whatever Barbara Levinson did or didn't do for her elderly mother, she felt guilty. First, her mother, Marion, fell and broke her hip. Then she had intestinal surgery. Finally, she was diagnosed with lung cancer. Juggling her mother's needs with the demands of a newborn baby, Barbara joined her sister, Lynn Kanter-Levy, in caring for their mother before she died. But while Lynn accepted her own limitations, Barbara could not.

"My sister says we did enough and in reality we probably did. But I think, well, I could have let Mother stay at my house more often," says Levinson. "Maybe that would have made me feel I was doing everything possible. But at the time—after 14 years of infertility and eight miscarriages—I just wanted to be with my newborn son. It all seemed overwhelming."

EVERYONE FEELS INADEQUATE

Levinson has plenty of company in trying to balance love, caregiving, and guilt. Some 52 million Americans care for a disabled or sick family member, according to a 1999 survey conducted by the U.S. Department of Health and Human Services. And although most bear their burden with love, social workers say caregiving is so demanding that most people feel inadequate.

Beware of guilt, experts warn. Eventually, such emotions can extract a heavy toll on the health of the caregiver—and that hurts everyone involved.

Of all the emotional hurdles family caregivers face—including anger and resentment—guilt is the most pervasive, says Mimi Goodrich, a licensed clinical social worker at the Wellness Center in San Mateo, California. "It's right up there on the list," she says. "The caregivers feel it's their obligation to make these years the happiest. But none of us has that power. When caregivers have expectations that are unrealistic, that's when the guilt comes in."

THE SUPERWOMAN SYNDROME

To make matters worse, people caring for a sick parent often find it difficult to ask for help or parcel-out tasks to friends or professionals. As with Levinson, the voice of the responsible child whispers in our minds: "She raised me. I should take care of her now, no matter how hard it is."

"People feel guilt because they think that somehow there's something they could, might, should, would have done," says Lee L. Pollak, director of the Bereavement Center at Jewish Family and Children's Services in San Francisco. "But the perfect ending never happens, no matter how well prepared a family is."

Pollak says America's goal-oriented, independent-minded society works indirectly to boost feelings of guilt. "We think we ought to be able to control things. So there's an extra layer of guilt if it doesn't go the way we want or expect."

GUILT HURTS

Caregivers need to cut themselves some slack, experts say, or their own health may suffer. Researchers at Indiana University, for instance, recently surveyed 3,000 women. They found that the longer women cared for a sick relative, the more likely they were to suffer depression, insomnia, and even physical difficulties climbing stairs or lifting heavy objects. The study was published in the March, 2000 issue of the *Journal of Health and Social Behavior*.

What can caregivers do to protect both themselves and their loved ones? Most importantly, turn to community programs and professional resources for help, as well as to family or friends. "Guilt is driven, in part, by the lack of access to information, especially during a crisis," says Pat Coleman, an elder-care consultant and founder of the web site Eldergift.com. "It's brought on by trying to get through the morass of needs and decisions and not knowing what supports and services are available. Often there hasn't been anyone there to tell us what we might need until we actually need it, so there's tremendous guilt in feeling we haven't done enough."

Consider also joining a support group—either in person or on the Internet—so you can share feelings and frustrations with others who understand your situation. And make sure to acknowledge your limits; you can say "no" without closing your heart. Some caregivers let go of their old life, and learn that their new life, though difficult, is still full of rewards. Others let go of control, and learn to delegate caregiving chores to others. No matter which choice you make, Pat Coleman offers this advice: "Remember that your best is good enough."

It's taken Barbara Levinson the three years since her mother died to truly learn that lesson. Her baby son is now a rambunctious preschooler. She knows he needed time with her. "If I had done things for my mother that made the rest of my life not make sense, maybe then I would have been doing enough for her," Levinson says, "but I wouldn't have been doing enough for my child—or for me."

In the second part of An Interview with Alzheimer's Caregivers, which follows, James and Joyce discuss the burdens which caring for Joyce's mother has placed on them, the sacrifices that they have had to make, and the services that help them in caring for Ella. Renaissance conduct books often suggest that there is a simple distinction between good, loving children who care for their aging parents and continue to treat them with love and reverence, and ungrateful children who neglect their elderly parents or show them a lack of respect. However, the interview below, like the article above, suggests that the adult child's role in caring for an elderly parent is a very complicated one, which involves balancing a variety of needs and considerations. Loving, responsible children will need at times to take on the role of parenting their parents, but they will also want to treat their parents with dignity and respect whenever possible. And children caring for their parents will also need to take into account the effect that the caregiving will have on their own lifestyles and on those of their spouses and children. Often they will feel guilty that they are not doing enough, or they may resent the amount of responsibility they are forced to bear. Like Edgar, who deceives his father in order to save him from despair, modern caregivers will have to find a balance between giving their "child-changed" parents the guidance and parenting that they now need and treating them with the respect that elderly parents deserve. And like Cordelia, who refuses to falsely flatter her father at the beginning of the play but later returns to rescue and forgive him, modern caregivers will have to find a balance between attending to their own needs and attending to the needs of their parents.

AN INTERVIEW WITH ALZHEIMER'S CAREGIVERS: PART II

Joyce, because you are your mother's only living child, a lot of the burden of caring for her falls on you. Are other family members helpful and supportive?

Joyce: My daughter who lives nearby is when she has time. She's also raising a daughter, and she's working full time, and she has a husband and a long commute.

And I feel like her first priority should be her husband and daughter. So I try not to ask her for help any more than I have to. But when I've asked for it she's always been willing. Like at Christmas time, she and her husband went to great lengths to take Mom out at Christmas.

And for a while Mom lived on her own near her sisters, but there were some things that happened that I really needed to be there with her more than her sisters because I could be stricter with her more than her sisters could be. I was up there once. I tried to take her to all her doctors' appointments, and I was up there once for a doctor's appointment after she'd broken her hip. And the doctor wanted to have her take a bone scan because he wanted to check her for osteoporosis. And so I wasn't going to be there at that time, so I made the appointment and told her sister that she needs to go for this to be checked. And mother was so worried about this. She thought it was going to be painful. She was so scared of a bone scan. So she talked her sister into canceling it after I left. Well, of course, after she got here she fell off the bed one day and then had a back ache for a long time after and finally I got her to a doctor who said she had a fracture in her lower spine caused by osteoporosis. That's when she was put on Fosamax. And it makes me furious when I think about it, because probably she wouldn't have had that if she had been on Fosamax the whole time, which she would have been if she had had the bone scan.

When your mother couldn't live on her own anymore, she stayed with you for a couple of months. Was that difficult?

Joyce: We had her with us for about two months after she came out of the convalescent hospital after she broke her hip. It was really difficult because we just didn't have any life of our own. I couldn't go anyplace, really. You try things like, I had a neighbor who said, "Well, I'll watch her any time you need." So I said, "If you could... I think she'll be O.K. I'm going to be gone for about an hour and I've done everything for her and she'll just be in her bed. I just need someone who's going to be here in case she needs somebody. She has your phone number." At that time mother could still dial the phone and she was pretty lucid. All she would really need help with is if she needed to get up to go to the bathroom, and I didn't think she was going to need to do that. So I thought everything was O.K., just so there was somebody she could call, the lady across the street here. And she assured me that would be just fine. Well, I got home and called to tell her that I was back, and she wasn't even there. She had gone to the store. So, I just didn't call that person anymore. And I find that, and other people have told me this before, it's easier to get a babysitter than to get somebody to sit with a senior citizen. It's really hard to get somebody who wants that responsibility. We tried for two months, and besides just not having any privacy and having this constant responsibility, and feeling I couldn't even go someplace hardly, she needed the heat so high in here, I found poor James out in the back yard just so he could breath once. And things like, James and I enjoy, on a warm day, opening the windows and letting the wind blow in and letting the curtains blow. That really shook her up. Her eyes were big and she had her hands up, and she was really scared because the curtains were blowing in. Food, I tried to have food that she would eat rather than food that we really enjoyed. So all these things were very difficult, and yet I know a lot of people are successful in combining the generations like this. I think maybe it might be a little more difficult with Mother than it would be with some other people because she had such odd ideas of how to eat and so on. In some ways, though, it would be easier than with some people because she wasn't difficult. She was really trying to be cooperative because she was hoping... even when we brought her back here when we knew that she was not going to be able to live by herself she was hoping that she would live with us rather than going to an "old people's home" as she called it. She was really fighting that. But it just wouldn't have worked out.

Joyce, you are a painter, and James, you were still working. When your mother was living with you, did having her with you interfere with your painting or your work?

Joyce: I don't think I got any painting done while she was here, that I recall.

James: You didn't.

Joyce: I don't think I got any done. I had a friend that I used to go painting with who did not understand my situation at all even though I tried to explain it to her. Her husband and daughter were out of state temporarily, and she was working here, and she thought that she could just come over on her days off or that she and I could go someplace. That just didn't work out at all. She just didn't understand that I didn't have that freedom anymore. Finally one day I let her come over to my place for a little bit, but I don't really have room for her to paint here. I think she and I did a little bit of painting in my studio, but really, hardly enough to matter. I think I showed her some things and she went home and finished it. Some people just don't understand how time-consuming caregiving is, and some people just don't understand about family responsibilities. And I didn't get much of anything done.

You've talked about having to make decisions for her. How do you make decisions about her care? What guides your decisions?

Joyce: I talk to doctors and to people like the director at the assisted-living home who have had a lot of experience with Alzheimer's people. Some of the nurses, I feel, have better information and advice than some of the doctors who might have more education but haven't had more hands-on experience. And I've made most of my decisions by really researching it as best as I can. I've found that I've gotten good help by going to this caretakers class that I took, "Taking Care of You," and from other people who have Alzheimer's people in their family, and finding out what my options are. That's about the only way I know to make decisions. In one case I made a decision based a lot on what I thought she would have wanted when she was able to make those decisions. For instance, I found out about these three drugs that the specialist told us may slow down Alzheimer's, may, if they work at all, keep people out of the Alzheimer's care place by six months, if they work at all. Then I came back and spoke with the director at the assisted-living place who used to be the director of an Alzheimer's unit. And she told me also that Vitamin E works about as well as those drugs and has no side effects, and I made the decision to go with that because I felt that that was the decision my mother would have made when she was able to make a decision because she always wanted to do things the natural way, as much as possible. So that's the only way I know to do it.

Has caring for her been a financial burden?

James: Not a burden, no. There's been some finances involved in it, but it's not a financial burden. It's more of a burden of being limited in what you are allowed to do. You can't travel. You can't be gone for a long period of time. But she has sufficient funds at this time to meet her own needs. So it really isn't a financial burden. She gets a V.A. pension and a little bit of social security, and the money that she got from selling her home we have put into various CDs, where she's earned interest on them, so we're not having to pay any out-of-pocket expenses for her. We probably give her a dollar each Sunday to put into the church offering, and I gave up trying to let her have her own stamps so I put stamps on things for her, but it isn't a financial burden.

Joyce: One problem we've noticed at the assisted-living home is that Mother was always used to having money all the time, and I felt it was best, mostly because it was hard for her to write a check out, I just would leave cash with her. Well, the cash started disappearing, and unfortunately I don't think it can be a resident. I think that it has to be a caretaker that was taking the money. And I did complain once about it, but they have no way of knowing who it could be. I can't even prove that it was happening for sure because Mother is a person who would probably give a person the shirt off her back if she thought they needed it. But I don't think that's what happened. I really think money was disappearing. So, we have a fund there for her, and anytime she needs money while we're gone all she has to do is ask for it. I used to, when I couldn't leave $40 with her anymore, I thought, well, I'll just leave her $3. The $3 disappeared. I never have found any objects disappearing, but the cash disappears right out of her purse. So, I just don't leave any cash with her whatsoever, which I feel kind of bad about because I know

Dad wanted her to have her own money, and shopping is something that she got a great deal of pleasure out of. But if I take her shopping now I just give her money when I get there, or I tell her, "Anything you want, tell me, and I'll write a check for you" because I keep her checkbook separate. And when we go to church on Sunday she always asks me for a dollar. And I feel like I'm treating her like a little kid, and I don't want to do that, but I don't see any reason to be giving money to somebody else who is stealing it.

James: Now one of the things that I noticed when I think about this is that over a period of time, when we first used to take her out to lunches she would say, "Well, I want to pay for this," or "I want to pay part of this," or if we would have to drive her up to someplace she would say, "Here's $10 for gas." Well of course it cost more than $10, but she was thinking of it. That no longer even enters her mind.

Joyce: She doesn't have any access to money anymore. She doesn't even think about money. Occasionally she'll say, "Well I want to help with this, too." She does do that once in a while still, but not as often.

James: Not as often, no.

What compromises or sacrifices or changes in your lifestyle have you had to make to take care of your mother?

Joyce: I go over to see her almost every day. Sometimes I skip a day, but not very often. One week I skipped three days and she went into a depression.

James: Sometimes you go three times a day.

Joyce: Yeah, I have. I try not to. It seems like it's getting more and more instead of less. It does limit our travel, especially on holidays. I would love to visit the rest of the family for Christmas, but…this last time we went out-of-state and spent Christmas with some other family, and our daughter and son-in-law who live nearby took her out and I'm sure that she had a nice Christmas because of them, but it seemed like it really did take advantage of them. I can't believe all they had to go through because it was so cold and they didn't have a heater in the car.

James: Because you can't get her into just any car. She couldn't get into their van.

Joyce: Then we had to come back earlier than I would have liked to have because her apartment that we'd been waiting for that was less expensive and closer to things became available right at Christmas time. They wanted us to move her right then, but we talked them into letting us wait till we could get back.

It's affected our travel plans. We aren't out traveling like maybe we'd like to spend our retirement doing. It's a lot worse for other people than it is for us, though. I realized that when I took that caretakers class. There are people that are much more tied down than we are. Mostly the ones who have them right in their homes are extremely tied down, and in order to even get away at all for a day or just overnight they have to get someone who will come in and stay in the home.

James: Joyce has given up certain kinds of organizations that she's been involved in that she got a certain amount of pleasure in, participating in the event center.

Joyce: Dog-walking at the Humane Society.

James: And she's got so she only paints with the plein air painters once a week instead of twice a week, so those things have been limited. And of course, sometimes I feel kind of neglected because she's always with her mother. But I realize how petty that is when I think about it, but nevertheless sometimes I feel that way.

And because we take Mom to church on Sunday morning, it limits the time that we can go to church, because she can't be there for too long. There's a first service, there's a Sunday school, and there's a second service. We just go to that one service. That's it.

Joyce: We don't go to the adult Sunday school class, even though that's sort of a social time. We would meet other people there, have coffee with them and stuff. We have friends in there. It would be nice to go to that. We used to go to that. But we found that it was kind of a big hassle because we would go to that. I would have to leave about ten minutes before it was over with, right about at the most interesting part, maybe, to go and pick up Mom, because she just wouldn't be able to sit through that. At one time, in fact, when we were taking her in the walker she had to leave several times in the middle of church, and that's why I went and got the wheelchair because she could not sit through church on the benches anymore.

James, for you, has there been a problem with not being able to see your dad because you need to be here with your wife and helping her with her mother?

James: Yes, Definitely. Definitely. That has been a problem.

Joyce: The family is spread out now.

James: That is why I finally said last Christmas, we're going to go to southern California. I'm going. You can stay here with your mother if you want, but I'm going.

Because you needed to see him?

James: Right, and I wanted to see my grandsons, and my other daughters, and I wanted to be down there. But I don't think we can justify doing that again this year. But I'm going to go down and see my dad on his birthday. I don't know whether Joyce will be able to go or not.

Joyce: I'm going to try. I'll just have to see how things are at that time. It's a lot easier though when it is not a holiday, because that puts such a burden on our daughter up here.

James: And this week coming up we're going on a family reunion, and so we'll be gone and our daughter and her family will be gone, and it has caused Joyce nothing but concern about what's going to happen on family night, and what's going to happen on . . . even though Ella's in the assisted-living home probably getting the best possible care that she could get, Joyce feels guilty just going on a family reunion. She really feels guilty about it, and I can understand a little bit why she does, but she needs some time to go and enjoy herself, and I need some time.

A lot of caregivers experience guilt that they are not doing enough, even though realistically they are doing all they can do. Has that been a problem for you?

Joyce: Oh sure, I don't think there is any way of getting around it.

Others talk about feeling resentment of the person that they have to care for because of the sacrifices that it involves. Has that been an issue for you?

Joyce: Well, it's probably not as bad for me as it would be for me if she was in my home. But there have been times when because of her demands I felt resentment, for instance about family night. Of course, now that she has been diagnosed as having Alzheimer's, I understand a little bit more. But there was a while there where it was just really hard for me to understand why she was so demanding. We have been to every family night except maybe two that we haven't been to, and one of those our daughter and son-in-law went to for us. And most of the people there never have people come to them for family night. But she thinks that the end of the world has come if we aren't there for every family night. And the one time that we couldn't make it she was calling up asking, "Can you come? Can you come?" and I had told her we couldn't come. And she said, "Well, I thought maybe you could come after all." And finally I did get mad at her. I told her, "You're spoiled."

James: Where I resent things is, we get to wherever we're going to be to take her early, and she's already mad at us because we're late. And I just have a really hard time with that. I understand that she thinks we're late, and it's real to her, but I have a really, really hard time with it, that she thinks we're late and she's mad at us, and so she doesn't even enjoy family night because we didn't get there until 4:45 and we weren't scheduled to be there till 5:00, but some people came at 4:00, because they have two different times.

I also sometimes feel like my retirement has been cheated. But when I start to resent her, I remember Exodus 20:12: "Honor your Father and Mother, that your days may be long upon the earth."

What services are available or do you take advantage of to help you?

Joyce: The head nurse at Spruce point told me about this class for caretakers called "Taking Care of You." It was a four- or five-day class, and I really did get a lot out of it. And I'm going to be taking another class called, "The Best Friend's Approach to Alzheimer's," which is what I had really asked questions about, how to approach and how to handle these people. Because they have some theories about this, and I see them working. I take her at least once a week to an Alzheimer's respite. And they really know how to handle the people. I see them talking to Mother and sitting right next to Mother and singing with her. There's an Alzheimer's support group that people who have some family member with Alzheimer's can go to once a month. It is helpful to talk to other people who are going through these experiences. There are all kinds of situations that you hear about. I realized that I have it really good compared to some of the other people.

And you've mentioned an Alzheimer's respite?

Joyce: Yes, it's been meeting twice a week but now it is going to be meeting three times a week. The people who go there are given a meal, and they all eat lunch together. They have crafts, music, activities. It costs about $10 each time, which kind of adds up. So I stopped taking Mom to every meeting and just take her to the one on the day when the activity director at her home is off. At first mom just loved it, now she says she doesn't enjoy it that much, but I get her to go anyway because I know it's better than sitting at home and wondering what she's going to do.

James: But it relates back to one of your other questions. Joyce has to take her, so that requires time. Joyce's back is bad, so that means that I've got to go to get the wheelchair into the car, and then later that afternoon go back, so there's a four-hour period in between. The thing is designed primarily to stimulate these people but to give the caregiver a four-hour break. That's the respite. But it then requires us to be tied down that day to take her there and to pick her up, and so it's a respite for people who care for them full time all by themselves, but for us it's just an extra trip.

James, what has your role been in caring for your wife's mother? And would you say that there are additional difficulties in caring for someone who isn't your parent?

James: I haven't ever really experienced caring for a parent, so I can't say if it's different. I can see that it wears on my wife, and that concerns me. I think that's my biggest concern. When she's doing so much she feels like she's not doing enough.

What advice would you give to caregivers to keep them from burning out or getting to the point where they are depriving themselves?

Joyce: Well, if you can possibly afford it, don't try to do it all yourself. I think I would have burned out long before this if I had tried to keep her in my home. That would be the main thing. And I think it would be very hard on our marriage. I don't think we'd have any kind of a life. In the class that I took, they stressed that it is very important for caretakers to at least every week write down a goal of doing something for yourself. Not something you should do. And not something that somebody needs to have you do for them, but something that you want to do. And I was already pretty well doing that with my art, but it was nice to hear it, though, that I was doing the right thing. And I saw people in the class that did not have this. Usually the people who have to take care of the parent in their home. Or like the person who was taking care of her husband in her home and had to give up her tax service that she had built up because he just required so much attention. So they really talked about this, how important it is to do something recreational, even if you have to get away a little bit. It is even good to get away a little bit, at least once or twice a week. They had us fill out papers and answer questions like "What are you going to do for yourself this week? When are you going to do this?" And then they had us report back as to whether we did it.

Are there rewards to caring for your mother?

Joyce: Well, satisfaction, I guess would be the only thing I can think of offhand. I promised my father I'd take care of her. And of course I would anyway. Satisfaction, fulfilling our responsibility, that's the main thing I would say.

MUSIC THERAPY

In act four of *King Lear,* music is used in an attempt to restore Lear's health and sanity, and in early modern England music was sometimes believed to be a cure for madness. As the article below demonstrates, music therapy is still employed today, and can be beneficial in helping Alzheimer's patients. In Shakespeare's day it was thought by some physicians that music could restore harmony to a mind or body that was out of harmony. Today, many nurses, physicians, and caregivers find that music helps to restore happiness and interest in life in Alzheimer's patients, while also helping to stimulate their appetites and to improve their hydration.

STEPHANIE SMITH, "MUSICIAN HELPS ALZHEIMER'S
PATIENTS"

By Stephanie Smith. CNN.Com, December 27, 2001
http://www.cnn.com/2001/HEALTH/conditions/12/26/alzheimer's.music/

WEST PALM BEACH, Florida (CNN)—The boom-bip and rat-a-tat-tat of songs like "Ain't She Sweet" and "When the Saints Come Marching In" ring through the air. Tony Sanso, a leftover of the ragtime music era, sweat glistening on his brow, is banging on the keys of a piano, while his audience, captivated, dances in front of him.

It may sound like a party, but actually it's a Thursday morning therapy session at the Alzheimer's/dementia ward of the Morse Geriatric Center.

"It's like a senior citizen Woodstock," Sanso said.

In some ways, it is. The cool, white halls of the Morse Center, though a far cry from the smoky lounges and clubs Sanso used to play, provide a musical focal point for this older generation. His music may do something for them that nothing else can.

Geriatric Circuit

The scene at the Morse Clinic is almost dreamy, quiet. Before Tony enters the room, the residents mill around, some moaning. Their faces are listless, their eyes glistening under the haze of Alzheimer's disease.

Until Sanso arrives.

"When Tony comes in, the room fills up and they know he's there," says Michelle Capogrosso, director of therapeutic recreation at Morse. "It's fun, it's light, it's lively. The music starts, they're singing, there's clapping. Even the staff is involved."

But this isn't just about fun and games. According to Capogrosso, there is a therapeutic benefit to this "party."

"The music really enhances their lifestyle, their quality of life," she says.

Dr. Juergen Bludau, the medical director at Morse, has seen immense benefits for residents there after Tony's routine.

"We've noticed that [the music] helps with hydration, it makes them thirsty, it makes them willing to drink," says Bludau. "It helps them . . . get to bed better. We are able to stimulate an appetite. So, it definitely has a positive impact on these patients."

Can music spark a dormant interest in life? Perhaps so.

A study on the impact of music therapy on dementia patients, conducted by Eastern Michigan University, determined that patients consumed 20 percent more calories when music was played during lunchtime—food for thought, certainly.

The Alzheimer's Association also lists music therapy as a potentially enriching activity. Music, it says, can stir memories and encourage group activity through singing and clapping.

The Association and the Michigan study caution, however, that the tunes must match the musical tastes of the residents—otherwise it could be harmful.

"They don't relate to Bon Jovi," says Sanso. "These people have lived a long time. . . . I gotta do their thing, their music, you know."

A Storied Career

He is qualified to play their golden oldies. A regular on the ragtime circuit in the 1950s, Sanso would mix slapstick comedy with music—what he called "ironic satire"—playing nightclubs in Atlantic City and New York.

Yet performing got to be more of a challenge with nearly every show, Sanso recalls. "I started to notice, like during the show, there'd be blank spots when I'd be singing, it would like go dead, for just a split second," says Sanso.

He went to doctors, who found bumps resembling chicken skin on his throat. Throat cancer, they said. Six years ago, he had a tracheotomy, and a career born under the lights came to an end under a knife. He'd never sing again, Sanso's doctor said.

But he could still play.

"Music is my life, and when cancer took my voice, I wanted to do something meaningful and productive," said Sanso. "What I'm doing now is much more meaningful and more spiritual than anything I've done before."

Sanso's efforts have paid off at More Geriatric Center, says Capogrosso.

"[The residents] think they're in their 20s or their 30s," she said. "They're able to remember the words of the songs, so when their families come here there is a bond where there wasn't any existing before."

"I KNOW NOT WHERE I DID LODGE LAST NIGHT": HOUSING OPTIONS FOR THE ELDERLY

When Lear decides to abdicate the throne, he informs Regan and Goneril that he and his hundred knights will stay with each of them by turns. When they begin to strip him of the "name and all the additions to a king," which he had reserved, and to deprive him of his hundred knights, he wanders out into the storm and his only shelter is a hovel provided by Gloucester. After he is taken to Dover he confesses, "I know not where I did lodge last night" (4.7.69–70). While Lear's situation is extreme, it is true that an aging parent in Shakespeare's day would have had few housing options available to him. If he were no longer capable of caring for himself then he would have to rely on his children or family members to take him in, or he might be declared lunatic and made a ward of the court, in which case the quality of his housing and care would depend entirely on the quality of the guardian the court appointed him.

Modern families have options available to them that were not available in Shakespeare's time. Nursing homes, retirement communities, and assisted-living homes can provide medical care and assistance with daily tasks, and they can also provide stimulating activities such as music and exercise. However, modern families also face problems that were not common in Shakespeare's time. Modern families are often spread out over greater geographic distances than the families in Shakespeare's time, and this makes caring for aging parents all the more difficult since it may involve either moving one member of the family or attempting to care for the parent from a distance. Although retirement homes, assisted-living homes, and other housing communities for the elderly provide modern families with some resources which were not available in Shakespeare's day, they also present some new difficulties since families must search for a housing situation that will best meet the physical and emotional needs of all family members, while not exceeding the family's financial resources. The next three documents explore some of the options available to families today, and some of the questions and issues that families should consider when making a decision about where an aging parent should live.

MODERN CONDUCT BOOKS

We no longer have conduct books of the type available in the sixteenth and seventeenth centuries, but many organizations do put out information sheets for families and caregivers of the elderly. However, while Renaissance conduct books emphasized children's duty to care for their aging parents, no matter what, modern fact sheets are more likely to caution family caregivers against completely sacrificing their own happiness or that of their spouses or children in an effort to care for their parents. The following excerpts from a Family Caregiver Alliance fact sheet provide guidelines to help family members make the difficult decision of what to do when an elderly family member can no longer live alone. The first excerpt [1] recommends that all family members, including the elderly parent, should be involved in open discussions about the new living situation and the changes in lifestyle that this living situation may cause for different family members. This sort of discussion, of course, did not take place when Lear informed his daughters that he would be living with them. The second excerpt [2] suggests that children caring for their parents should keep in mind their past experiences with their parents and should not allow themselves to feel obligated to sacrifice their own happiness or that of other family members in order to care for their parents. Again, this is the sort of advice that was not offered in Shakespeare's day and was certainly not offered to Lear's family.

EXCERPTS FROM THE FAMILY CAREGIVER ALLIANCE FACT SHEET: *HOME AWAY FROM HOME: RELOCATING YOUR PARENTS* (2003)

Family Caregiver Alliance, San Francisco, CA,
http://www.caregiver.org/caregiver/jsp/content_node.jsp?nodeid=849

[1] Open and honest discussion with your parent and other family members becomes an essential first step when you are trying to decide whether relocating your parent is the right thing to do. Family meetings with your parent, spouse, children, siblings and other key people will help everyone share their views and will help you decide how best to proceed. Active communication among all family members is the building block to a strong support system for an older parent and all family members involved.

Although some of these discussions may be very difficult and emotional, several topics require attention. Together, the family, including your parent, will need to talk about all possible residential options, each person's role in the transition, the type of care to be provided, changes in lifestyle, finances, and the physical setting of the new home. Clear expectations must be defined.

[2] Families are rich in historical experiences, and many of your positive and negative feelings about your parents and other family members will play a role in your decision to relocate or live with a parent. Be honest with yourself and do not allow unresolved conflicts or feelings of guilt or obligation pressure you into taking on more than you can manage.

- Be honest with yourself and others about the significant life changes that relocating your parent will mean for you, your parent, your siblings, your spouse, and children.
- Try to come to terms with past disagreements between you and your parent.
- When deciding whether to relocate or move your parent into your home, consider the opinions of your spouse, children, siblings, and other family members.
- Come to an agreement with your siblings regarding how much and what kind of help you will receive from them.

The following article discusses a housing option which was not available in Shakespeare's time, and which is not even widely available today. It is a healthcare facility for Alzheimer's patients, but it differs from many such facilities in that it offers a community setting in which patients feel at home and it allows patients to continue to feel that they are responsible, contributing members of the community by giving them the responsibility of caring for plants and animals. By doing this, the home helps to combat the feeling of powerlessness that plagues Lear. Such a setting might have been more beneficial for Lear than his "reservation of an hundred knights" (1.1.133). He might have been better-off continuing to feel important and productive rather than seeking to "unburthened crawl toward death" (1.1.39).

LORI BURLING, "HEALTH CARE FACILITY TAKES NEW APPROACH FOR DEMENTIA PATIENTS"

By LORI BURLING, Associated Press Writer. February 28, 2003, The Associated Press State and Local Wire. Reprinted with the permission of the Associated Press.

Louisville, Ky.

Suzanne "Granny" McCord sat with a smile in the mall attached to her new living center that will house residents with Alzheimer's disease.

"Good morning, Ms. McCord," a staffer waved as he walked through the corridor Thursday morning.

McCord has lived in the Episcopal Church Home for nearly two years. Next week, she will move to the new $7.1 million Memory Care Center of Excellence, designed to care for dementia patients using a method of care that is designed to provide patients a home-like community instead of a hospital-like environment.

It's more than just a care center because it offers a beauty salon, a gift shop and a pet store where residents can check out animals like library books.

"I just love it here," she said Thursday during the grand opening of the center.

The Eden Alternative method was developed by geriatric physician William Thomas. The concept of the program is to surround the Alzheimer's patient with living things—such as plants and pets—and provide social opportunities and a sense of purpose. The facility—designed as eight separate communities equipped with bedrooms, living rooms, and kitchens—is centered on the mall area where residents can feel like they are in a community instead of a nursing home.

"It's more like living in a single dwelling than an institution," said Keith Knapp, CEO of Episcopal Church Home, which owns the center. "Just because you have Alzheimer's disease does not mean you should be disconnected with the community. We're encouraging residents to take responsibility of taking care of a pet or plant to give them the satisfaction of doing something meaningful to another living thing."

Knapp said the 52-room center is the first in the state that was built as a care center based solely on the Eden method. It's one of about 120 throughout the country according to Knapp. Facilities that use the program must also have specially trained staff.

No definitive numbers of these types of communities are available because the National Alzheimer's Association does not keep track of Eden Alternative facilities.

According to the Eden Alternative's Web site, many care facilities or nursing homes throughout the country have trained staff in Eden's approach. There is only one other center in Kentucky, but it is not solely devoted to dementia residents.

"In Jefferson County, there are nine nursing homes that have units for Alzheimer's care, but they are not all licensed for the same levels of care," said Alison Serey, president and CEO of the Alzheimer's Association of the Greater Kentucky and Southern Indiana Chapter.

The new center will also be used as a research and training facility for students and faculty at the University of Louisville and the University of Kentucky.

"We want to teach residents (graduate students) to be good physicians in caring for patients with memory loss," said Karen Robinson, a professor of U of L's School of Nursing.

Graham Rowles, an associate director of UK's Sanders-Brown Center on Aging, who has done extensive research on Alzheimer's, said the facility will provide a new style of research.

"Research that works for people," Rowles said. "Faculty and students will be able to talk with people who are memory impaired and how this approach is helping them. Does having a flower shop or a pet store close make a difference?"

Charles Pierce, whose father lived with the disease for four years before his death in 1989, said the mall activities will certainly make a difference.

"They have a disease. They haven't gone crazy," said Pierce, of Boston, who wrote the book *Hard To Forget: An Alzheimer's Story*. "This is the kind of facility I had hoped for for my dad."

Suzanne McCord's daughter-in-law, Susan McCord, said she has been anticipating an Eden facility for a long time.

"Had they had this facility five years ago my mother, Martha Hill, would have been here too," said Susan McCord, whose mother is in the late stages of Alzheimer's and is staying at an adjacent nursing home. "This place is family-oriented, and my mother would have loved the flower area."

The long-term care facility, which costs residents $145 a day, is equipped with a locked courtyard and gardening areas. Each of the four wings contains living areas and multiple bedrooms. Those residents share laundry and kitchen facilities. Each living area was built using special technology and memory enhancement concepts, such as decorating each living area with a different theme.

"If a resident gets turned around, he can tell a staff member, 'I live in the horse area,'" Knapp said referring to the living quarters decorated in thoroughbred paraphernalia.

Knapp said the program is simply designed to curb three things: loneliness, helplessness, and boredom.

"It's a social magnet," he said. "It focuses more on what they (residents) want to do, rather than something planned for them to do."

AN INTERVIEW WITH ALZHEIMER'S CAREGIVERS: PART III

While facilities like the one mentioned above are a wonderful resource for those who live near to them, they are not always widely available. In the final section of the interview with James and Joyce, they discuss some of the housing options they have considered and tried for Ella and those that they may have to try in the future. They have to consider which facilities would be able to meet Ella's medical needs, but they are also concerned about her emotional needs and her mental and physical stimulation, and, of course, they want a home that is close to them so that they can visit often. Once again James and Joyce have to find a way to care for Ella as though she were their child while treating her with the respect and dignity due to a parent. As the interview below demonstrates, modern families still face many difficult decisions when caring for an aging parent. Though there are more resources available now than in Shakespeare's day, there are also additional problems and the same age-old concerns.

You've mentioned that first Ella was living alone in California about half an hour from you, and then she was living up in Oregon near her sisters, and then she stayed with you. When those living situations didn't work out anymore, what did you consider or try?

James: We looked at just a regular retirement home. We looked at the assisted-living place, where she did settle on, and we looked at adult foster homes.

Joyce: I wasn't happy with any of the foster care places that I looked into. I only really saw one, but the ones I looked into, either they looked terrible on the outside or in interviewing people over the phone I wasn't very impressed. Some of them would have made Mom comply to standards that would have made her wear a different kind of Depends than she wanted to wear, or would have allowed smoking in some rooms, or some of them would not have allowed you to bring pets over to visit, and I sometimes bring pets over to visit. One that I interviewed that I knew that wouldn't be right for Mom at all was where the woman said, "Well, there's lots of activity here because I have people in to play cards all the time." And Mother does not like card games.

I did go to see another one, come to think of it. I looked at another foster home. It was very nicely decorated, but it looked to me like there was just nothing for her to do. But mostly there was a privacy issue. At most of them you couldn't have your own furniture and bring it in. You had to use their furniture that was already in there. Maybe you'd be allowed to have a favorite picture or something like that.

So it would mean giving up even more of her independence and her memories?

Joyce: Yeah, I wanted her to have as much of her own stuff as possible. And then when we tried the retirement home, I got a whiff of tobacco smoke as I was walking down the halls, and they do let people smoke in their own rooms.

James: And in that home they provide meals and of course you have your own room, but if you need additional things, as Ella has developed that she does, you have to hire somebody to take care of these needs. If you need somebody to help you with your medications, or with your bathing, or with your laundry, you had to hire somebody to do that. Whereas at the assisted living, that is built into it; now, there are various costs associated with it, but they provide those services, and that is why we felt that assisted living was better. Plus it was the nicest looking of the places.

Early on we realized that she needed help with her medications, too, because they would bring them into her and she wouldn't take them because she'd say that she'd already taken them.

Joyce: When we first started at the assisted-living home, she was only taking three medications, and to make sure that she was taking them I had her use these little weekly pillboxes. But one of the medications that she was taking, to keep off the TIAs, it is very important not to take two and not to skip. And a couple times I found that the ones for that day hadn't been taken, which really worried me, and I didn't know what to do at that point. I tried a couple of different things, but it just wasn't working, and so I had to turn that over to them. And I hated to do that because it was taking one more bit of freedom away from her. She'd always loved taking vitamins. She'd had cupboards full of them. But now that it has been turned over to them, she doesn't even enjoy taking pills anymore. But we had to give that over to them, and more and more things have happened like that. She just requires a lot more care than she used to require. And I'm glad we didn't put her in the retirement home.

Was your mother able to be involved in the decision about what sort of place to live, or did she just want to live with you and not consider any other options?

Joyce: She wanted to live with me, and I knew that wasn't going to work, so I just began visiting and looking into all these other things, mostly without consulting her or letting her know that I was looking because she was so closed on the subject. And after I visited these two places, and I was really impressed with the way the assisted-living home looked because it was so much prettier than the retirement home, which is an older building and just wasn't decorated as nicely, I told her I wanted her to go with me to visit the assisted-living home, and also we were going to have a lunch there. So we had lunch there and we walked her through with one of the staff members, and we looked at the one bedroom and the studio apartments. I could tell she wasn't accepting any of it. But she finally did say, "Well, if I was going to live in a place like this I'd just live in the studio apartment. I'd just take the studio apartment because I can't see the point of taking a one bedroom." And I said, "O.K." So I'm afraid I took advantage of the situation. And then it was about a month or more before she actually moved in because they have to go through being accepted and so on. In the meantime James thought it would really be better for her if she moved into a one bedroom. At that time she was still making her own bed and stuff, this is something she can't do anymore. And we thought it would be better for her to have two rooms there. But she would not even consider it. So at this time I talked to one of her sisters and asked her to talk to Mother about it, and her sister convinced her that she should have a place where she could take her own bed and so on.

You've mentioned activities. What sort of activities does the assisted-living home offer?

Joyce: Quite a variety, really. It all depends on who the activity director is. But with this present one they have a lot of very good activities. I always feel like they should have more than they do, but I think this one is doing about the best of anyone that I've seen. They have musical groups come in, and entertain them, and everyone enjoys that and my mother just loves it, especially the brass band, and the River City Rascals, which is a barbershop quartet. They had a group that the activity director just brought in, the Old Time Fiddlers, and that was a hoedown. That was really fun. I went to it with mom. These people are really talented and they had everybody clapping and participating.

Mother was even talking about it the next day she enjoyed it so much. Music seems to really reach them more than anything.

Cooking classes are very popular. A lot of them really enjoy doing cooking because they can't do cooking in their room because they aren't allowed to have a regular oven. They can only have a microwave. They can't have a regular stove.

The director has taken to taking them out on drives in the bus, at least once a week, just to get them out. They just drive around town. She takes them to see the pretty scenery. Today she had a picnic, and most of the people went to it. They took a couple of bus trips to get them there, and had a lot of help, I understand. The only thing is that because Mother is in a wheelchair and because she has to be watched pretty closely, if she's going to take Mom out of the bus then she wants me along, so then it means that I have to go to these things, too. I enjoy it. The time that I went with them on the bus trip I had a good time with them, but nevertheless it's one more thing that I have to do and one more thing away from James and away from my art and so on.

James: They have exercises.

Joyce: Yes, that's good. Fitness for fun. And they are really good exercises. They have them raising their arms up and down. She had them do things with paper plates that required coordination. I was worn out doing the exercises with them one day. I was amazed at how well they were doing. That was a workout, which was really good for them. And that's to music.

What other sorts of living situations, if it gets to the point where she can't stay there, would you have to consider?

Joyce: Well, she might have to go to a lockdown facility of some type. Her current home isn't a lockdown facility. They can come and go anytime they want to, all they ask of them is that they sign in and sign out so that if there's a fire they know how many people to look for. At a lockdown facility every patient wears an armband, and it alerts the door, so that when the patient comes near the door, the door automatically locks and can't be opened. Even if, say a patient happened to be standing near me, and I was somebody who had a legitimate reason for going through the door, the door wouldn't open. It's neat and everything, and clean. I went and looked through it. The rooms are very small, and there doesn't seem to be much to do there, it didn't seem like to me, and all the patients were in their housecoats. That would be one facility I would have to consider. I know people who are bringing their parents from out-of-state to live there, but the concern I hear is that there is not enough for them to do. Another option is that I might look again at foster homes to see if there is a place where she could get a lot of attention. There are Alzheimer's places outside of this town that are supposed to be pretty good, but that's at least half an hour away. So I wouldn't be able to see her as often. There is an excellent one where they have not only activities, but they have hair stylists and manicurists who come in and do their nails for them, and they have an area in the back where they are fenced in so they can't wander off, but it is so big that they don't even know they are fenced in, but that's a couple of hours away, so I wouldn't be able to see her very often.

ALZHEIMER'S: A FIRSTHAND ACCOUNT

Reading the stories of caregivers can help us to understand *King Lear* from another perspective, but it may not help us to understand what Alzheimer's is like for the person diagnosed with the disease. Much of the tragedy of *King Lear* comes from watching Lear's own descent into madness, and seeing him fight against his loss of control, so it is important to be able to imagine how he might have felt as he experienced the change in his judgment and personality. The following excerpts from Cary Smith Henderson's book, *Partial View: An Alzheimer's Journal,* document his own experiences with Alzheimer's disease. In an attempt to find a cure for disabling headaches and loss of vision, Cary Henderson, a history professor at James Madison University, underwent a brain shunt operation, and a biopsy taken during this operation allowed for an unusual early diagnosis of Alzheimer's disease, which normally cannot be definitively diagnosed while the patient is living. Faced with the diagnosis, Professor Henderson chose to chronicle his own experiences so that others could learn more about this disease. Though, unlike Lear, he was always cared for and assisted by loving family members, his experiences in many ways resemble those of Lear. Just as Lear prays, "Let me not be mad" (1.5.38) so Henderson feels "panic" at the thought of "losing [his] brains." And just as Lear thinks that he is dead when Cordelia and the physicians awake him (4.7.45–9), so Henderson refers to his life before Alzheimer's as "when I was alive." You will probably note other similarities as you read these excerpts from Henderson's book. Reading these excerpts from Henderson's journal may help you to sympathize with Lear, a "a poor, infirm, weak, and despised old man," who makes many mistakes, but who is also bravely struggling to cling to his identity as he is losing his mind (3.2.19).

FROM CARY SMITH HENDERSON, *PARTIAL VIEW: AN ALZHEIMER'S JOURNAL,* ED. JACK HENDERSON MAIN, RUTH D. HENDERSON, AND NANCY ANDREWS, PHOTOGRAPHS BY NANCY ANDREWS

(Dallas, Tex: Southern Methodist University Press 1998). Reprinted with permission of the Southern Methodist University Press.

I would like to be somebody who could help understanding from the patient's point of view—what it is like to be an Alzheimer's patient.

It's somebody's version of hell and I guess I'll someday have to write a book about that, which is exactly what I am trying to do. (4)

We have music to start off today with—this is Mahler's *Resurrection* symphony, which I dearly love. And it's a little bit loud, but sometimes, actually, I feel that way. I want to shout. I want to raise some hell. I want to be somebody I'm not.

The only real constant friend I've got is music. I don't have to worry too much—I just turn on the radio and—thank goodness I know how to turn the radio on—and turn it off—I'm not sure about turning it off, but I can turn it on. (17)

Very simply put, we are clumsy, we are forgetful, and our caregivers, of course, understand that, although sometimes I think it must be very hard on the caregivers too, very, very hard, because some of us, me for example, can be very, very stubborn. We want things to be like they used to be. And we just hate that, the fact that we cannot be what we used to be. It hurts like hell. (18)

Every time I have a feeling that I'm losing—losing contact, losing my brains, whatever it is, I panic. I think the really worst thing is you're so restricted, not so much by other people, but you just feel that you are half a person and you so often feel that you are stupid for not remembering things or for not knowing things. Believe me, no matter how much I might be writing on the subject or thinking on the subject, it still just gets my goat—just the knowledge that I've goofed again—I said something wrong or I feel like I did something wrong or that I didn't know what I was saying—that's one of the things—or I forgot—all of these things are just so doggone common they get your goat sometimes. (19)

I'd like a larger world than I have right now.

Very often I wander around looking for something which I know is very pertinent, but then after a while I forget all about what it was I was looking for. When I'm wandering around, I'm trying to touch base with anything, actually. (24)

I've been thinking about myself. Some time back, we used to be, I hesitate to say the word, "human beings." We worked, we made money, we had kids, and a lot of the things we did not like to do and a lot of things we enjoyed. We were part of the economy. We had clubs that we went to, like Kiwanis Club and Food Bank. I was a busy little bee. I was into all sorts of things, things that had to do with charities, or things that had to do with music. Just a lot of things I did back when I was, I was about to say—alive—that may be an exaggeration, but I must say this really is, it's living, it's living halfway.

But one thing is for sure. You never can be, never will be, what you once were. And that's hard to swallow. It certainly was for me. I was very busy in all sorts of things when I was alive, you might say. Then, just gradually, these things became impossible. So we must factor that in, I suppose, something that's going to be with us forever, as long as we live at least. It's either that or die, and dying is something that you have to plan for and want very much. I'm not much into dying right now—yet. (35)

QUESTIONS FOR WRITTEN AND ORAL DISCUSSION

1. Regan and Goneril note in the first scene that Lear's judgment is impaired and that as he gets older they will have to deal more often with his "unruly waywardness"

(1.1.296). If you think of Lear as having Alzheimer's, do you feel more sympathy for Lear? Do you feel more sympathy for his daughters?

2. Does Lear seem more or less heroic if you think of him as an old man suffering from dementia?

3. If Lear really is showing the "infirmity of... age" and impaired judgment, is he right to give up the throne?

4. In what ways do Lear's symptoms seem similar to those of the Alzheimer's or dementia patients described in this chapter? In what ways are his symptoms different? Look over the fact sheets from the National Institute on Neurological Disorders and Strokes. Which of these symptoms does Lear manifest?

5. While Regan, Goneril, and Edmund certainly do not appear to be very good caregivers, Cordelia and Edgar, with their unfailing devotion to the fathers who reject them, may be unrealistic role models for many children facing the challenge of caring for their parents. After reading the articles on caregivers, what advice would you give to Cordelia and Edgar to keep them from burning out or from sacrificing other important parts of their lives?

6. Look over the advice given in the excerpts from the Family Caregiver Alliance fact sheet, *Home Away from Home*, and consider the housing options described in this chapter. With those documents in mind, stage a discussion of the type recommended by the Family Caregiver Alliance between the members of Lear's family. Have students play the roles of Lear, Cordelia, Regan, Goneril, Albany, Cornwall, and possibly Kent and the Fool. What would each character have to say about Lear's proposed living situation? What might have been gained by such a discussion? Could the tragedy have been averted?

7. How is Cary Henderson's story similar to Lear's? What do the two men have in common?

8. Compare the use of music therapy in *King Lear* with its use in the geriatric center described in Stephanie Smith's article and the assisted-living center activities described in Part III of the Interview with Alzheimer's Caregivers. Are they similar? How could music help to soothe or enliven people?

9. How does music help Cary Smith Henderson? How does this use of music compare with its use in *King Lear?*

Index

About the Author

DONNA WOODFORD is Assistant Professor of English at New Mexico Highlands University.